**Thank you for
your contribution
to the RSPB's
Action for Birds**

Ian Prestt
Director General

For Love of Birds

The Story of the
Royal Society for the Protection of Birds,
1889-1988

by Tony Samstag

RSPB

Acknowledgements
I would like to thank Nick Hammond, RSPB Director (Information and Education), for commissioning me to write this book, Patsy Hinchliffe for designing it and Ian Dawson, RSPB Librarian, for meticulously checking the text and for generously sharing with me his encyclopaedic knowledge of the Society and its archives. I also thank the following publishers: *BBC Wildlife* magazine for quotations from 'Artists and Animals' by Nicholas Hammond; The University of California Press for material from *Feather Fashions and Bird Preservation* by Robin Doughty; Collins for extracts from *The Return of the Osprey* by Philip Brown and George Waterston; T & A D Poyser for extracts from *Enjoying Ornithology*, edited by Ron Hickling; Michael Joseph for quotations from *All Heaven in a Rage* by E S Turner; Elm Tree Books/Hamish Hamilton for the chapter from *Bird Detective* by Peter Robinson, and *The Times* for 'Where the joy of watching'.

Dedication
Sylvia vulgaris: they know who they are.

Published by the Royal Society for the Protection of Birds, The Lodge, Sandy, Bedfordshire SG19 2DL.

ISBN No 0 903138 28 X

Designed by Patsy Hinchliffe
Typesetting by Bedford Typesetters Ltd
Origination by Saxon Photolitho Ltd
Printing and binding by W S Cowell Ltd
Distribution by Christopher Helm (Publishers) Ltd

Foreword

With our 100th birthday in the offing we wanted to publish a book that would celebrate the Society's achievements. We did not, however, want a glib account that made the most of our successes and ignored our failures. Ours would have been a very strange Society if everything it had done had been successful. To have represented the Society in such a one-sided light would also have been a contradiction of our open-minded approach to the problems of bird conservation. We have long accepted that we cannot realistically regard all our tasks in black and white and, wherever possible, we seek the areas of grey where we can find agreement with those who favour a different approach. So, our history, too, must be presented with the tones of grey between the black and white.

To ensure a measure of objectivity we commissioned an author whose American birth, British nationality and Scandinavian residence give an international perspective to his undoubted knowledge of the conservation scene in the United Kingdom. And we gave him the Cromwellian instruction to paint us 'warts and all'. Those readers seeking uncritical adulation of the Society will, therefore, be disappointed, but the discerning reader will realise that 'warts and all' the RSPB is an organisation of which we can all be justly proud.

IAN PRESTT
Director General RSPB

The RSPB Seal

3

"If the day and night are such that you greet them with joy, and life emits a fragrance like flowers and sweet-scented herbs, is more elastic, more starry, more immortal – that is your success. All nature is your congratulation, and you have cause momentarily to bless yourself."

—Thoreau: Walden

The great auk, extinct 1844–45 – from Lost British Birds *by W H Hudson – RSPB Leaflet No 14.*

4

Contents

RSPB Christmas card 1900.

Photograph of The Aviary – a Bird Fancyers Recreation – printed handkerchief of the 1760s by J Laughton (donated to the RSPB in 1987 by Mrs Ita).

Various bird species are depicted around the edges, with notes on their capture and nurture. That on the robin reads, "Is Catch'd with a trap Cage and limesticks, he is very tender and has the Stagers but give him an earwig or a Spider and in his water some stick liquorish or saffron to prevent his eversinging".

The central illustration shows a boy birds-nesting. The lady is holding a cagebird and in the centre a clap net, with decoys, is in operation.

6

1. 'The Most Destructive Animal in the World'

Man as a species is born in sin, and conservationists are the high priests of a religion whose solitary premise is guilt. That guilt is the beating heart of the Royal Society for the Protection of Birds and all others of its ilk. Its more sanctimonious members should try never to forget that the mantle of responsibility they have assumed is reversible: they are among the saved, yes, but they are also the enemy, the devil incarnate, man the destroyer. Like it or not, it is their birthright.

The children at London Zoo enter a little cage marked 'The Most Destructive Animal in the World' and come face to face with a camera! The little old ladies in their hide on some stretch of swamp in the middle of nowhere watch horrified as a big bad heron scoffs a cuddly little duckling: "Can't somebody kill it?" they cry.

The RSPB is of this world, which is to say that it was born in and of cruelty, has thrived on it for a hundred years, grown prosperous and successful in fear, loathing and pain. Without the propensity of men, women and children to exercise their power as a species in a wantonly destructive way, the RSPB would go out of business. This is true of every environmental or conservationist body that has ever existed. Their futures, assuming that they do not succumb to the curse of amateurism, are secure. Even when one nation or another has pressed the final button, and man as a species has at last detonated himself back down the evolutionary scale to a less disproportionate position in the scheme of things, somebody, somewhere, will still be scurrying through the blasted ruins in search of whatever other lowly life form might have survived, to protect it for – and from – future generations.

The British public spends many millions of pounds annually in pursuit of wildlife, an escapist pursuit, that is, as opposed to a venereal, which of course it also is, in part – generating an enormous industry in the process: books (of which this is one); films, television series, radio programmes; charities (of which the RSPB is one) and learned bodies (of which the RSPB is also one) at an impressively high density for a country of this size; bad art on the walls and facile artefacts on mantelpieces and in the form of cheap and nasty jewellery, textiles, keychain fobs, abominations of taste beyond counting or description. Even the RSPB has made its contribution to this subculture of tat.

As a species, mankind, not to mention the British, is unique only in degree. What the wildlife-loving public tends to forget is that nature is not nice. An environment must be assumed hostile until proven otherwise. Then and only then can it be said to have become a habitat.

Those creatures that exist in a habitat, *inhabit* it, are said to 'survive'. Survival, whether of individuals, of species, of anything whatsoever that a natural scientist might consider a fit subject for census or taxonomy . . . or of any voluntary organisation, come to that, is always an achievement, never a mere fact of life. There is nothing natural about it. Killing and being killed are natural; death and decay are what living is all about. Anything that survives is bucking the system: surviving by definition on borrowed time.

When the fancies of men and women turn to nature, they leave their animal selves far behind. They forget what a hard-won luxury it is that they are indulging, how many other living things had to die so that human beings could draw breath, pause without fear, and admire the best or the worst the elements might throw at them. Other men and women died, too, so that these survivors could wallow in rhapsody while contemplating the view from their patch. Anyone who really believes that conservation is an end in itself should consider whether he or she was inclined to shed any tears over the extinction of the smallpox virus a few years ago – and if not, why not? And what is it about cuddly animals and pretty flowers (many of which, after all, are no less naturally inimicable to Man as a species) that makes them inherently any more cherishable than that?

The RSPB or the Society as we might as well call it, celebrates its centenary as a mere device. If we are to judge it, we can only do so, as a species like any other, in terms of self-interest. It is not the birds we cherish; it is ourselves.

All of the earliest conservation laws are explicit on that point. Animals and plants were for working, eating, medicinal treatment, industrial use. When Parliament turned its ponderous attention to the wellbeing of wildfowl, for example, as in 1533, the object of protecting their eggs and prohibiting their slaughter at certain times of year was to maintain an exploitable resource.

"It is clear", writes one historian of British nature conservation, "that concern for plants and animals was conditional on their being of direct value for man. Very little sympathy or interest was shown for wildlife itself."

The exploitative instinct led inevitably to that which we are pleased to call 'pure science', a spirit of inquiry whose ethical content is surely as questionable as in any other human endeavour; but there is no arguing the fact that the development of the natural sciences coincided with the first glimmerings of a humane approach to the rest of the animal kingdom. By the mid-nineteenth century the first recognisable natural history clubs and societies had formed, a mere century or so after the likes of the Aurelian Society and the Linnean Society of London, and 200 years after the founding of the Royal Society in 1660.

By 1854, a speaker at the inaugural dinner of the Wiltshire Archaeological and Natural History Society was deploring the "ignorance, superstition and the sheer love of cruelty" evident in the local attitude towards wildlife. Anger increased as pragmatic exploitation of wildlife was increasingly overshadowed by bloodlust, and the great sport-shooting parties made possible by eighteenth century firearms technology set their notorious records, with some individuals numbering their yearly 'bags' in the thousands. Others did not even bother to count, or to retrieve the dead and maimed.

With the fashion for plumage in the nineteenth century, cruelty to birds (albeit, this time, in the service of exploitation-as-usual) reached new heights. One MP described the plumage hunters at work during one of their *battues*, as the occasions were known, cutting the wings off living birds and "flinging the victims into the sea, to struggle

8

with feet and head until death came slowly to their relief". He had, he added, seen cliffs "absolutely spotted with the fledglings which had died of starvation".

In 1868 Professor Alfred Newton was moved to harangue the British Association at Norwich: "Fair and innocent as the snowy plumes may appear on a lady's hat, I must tell the wearer the truth – she bears the murderer's brand on her forehead."

It was public outrage at the atrocities perpetrated in the name of fashion that was to inspire the formation of the Society. But that was coincidence; there was no shortage of wildlife issues then as now, virtually any of which might have justified a campaign.

Such outrage was expressed by writers like John Galsworthy; whose *For Love of Beasts*, originally printed in the *Pall Mall Gazette*, was published as an RSPB leaflet, and a variation on which has provided the title of this book. Here is a short extract:

Before I could comment on my friend's narrative, we were spattered with mud by passing riders, and stopped to repair the damage to our coats.

"Jolly for my new coat!" I said. "Do you notice, by the way, that they are cutting men's tails longer, this spring?"

He raised those quizzical eyebrows of his, and murmured:

"And horses' tails shorter. Did you see those that passed just now?"

"No."

"There were none!"

"Nonsense!" I said; "My dear fellow, you really are obsessed about beasts! They were just ordinary."

"Quite – a few scrubby hairs, and a wriggle."

"Now, please," I said, "don't begin to talk of the cruelty of docking horses' tails, and tell me a story of an old horse in a pond."

"No," he answered, "I should have to invent it. What I was going to say was this: Which do you think the greater fools in the matter of fashion – men or women?"

"Oh! Women."

"Why?"

"There's always some sense at the bottom of men's fashions."

"Even of docking tails?"

"You can't compare it, anyway," I said, "with such a fashion as the wearing of 'aigrettes'. That's a cruel fashion if you like!"

"Ah! But you see," he said, "the women who wear them are ignorant of its cruelty. If they were not, they would never wear them. No gentlewoman wears them, now that the facts have come out."

"What is that you say?" I remarked.

He looked at me gravely.

"Do you mean to tell me," he asked, "that any woman of gentle instincts, who knows that the 'aigrette', as they call it, is a nuptial plume sported by the white egret only during the nesting season – and that, in order to obtain it, the mother birds are shot, and that, after their death, all their young die, too, from hunger and exposure – do you mean to tell me that any gentlewoman, knowing that, wears them? Why! most women are mothers themselves! What would they think of gods who shot women with babies in arms for the sake of obtaining their white skins to wear on their heads, eh?"

"But, my dear fellow," I said, "you see these plumes all about!"

"Only on people who don't mind wearing imitation stuff."

I gaped at him.

"You need not look at me like that," he said: "A woman goes into a shop. She knows that real 'aigrettes' mean killing mother-birds and starving all their nestlings. Therefore, if she's a real gentlewoman she doesn't ask for a real 'aigrette'. But still less does she ask to be supplied with an imitation article so good that people will take her for the wearer of the real thing. I put it to you, would she want to be known as an encourager of such a practice? You can never have seen a *lady* wearing an 'aigrette'."

"What!" I said: "What?"

"So much for the woman who knows about 'aigrettes'," he went on. "Now for the woman who doesn't. Either, when she is told these facts about 'aigrettes' she sets them down as 'hysterical stuff', or she is simply too 'out of it' to know anything. Well, she goes in and asks for an 'aigrette'. Do you think they sell her the real thing – I mean, of course, in England – knowing that it involves the shooting of mother-birds at breeding time: I put it to you: Would they?"

His inability to grasp the real issues astonished me, and I said:—

"You and I happen to have read the evidence about 'aigrettes' and the opinion of the House of Lords' Committee that the feathers of egrets imported into Great Britain are obtained by killing the birds during the breeding season; but you don't suppose, do you, that people whose commercial interests are bound up with the selling of 'aigrettes' are going to read it, or believe it if they do read it?"

"That," he answered, "is cynical, if you like. I feel sure that, in England, people do not sell suspected articles about which there has been so much talk and inquiry as there has been about 'aigrettes', without examining in good faith into the facts of their origin. No, believe me, none of the 'aigrettes' sold in England can have grown on birds."

"This is fantastic," I said. "Why! if what you're saying is true, then – then real 'aigrettes' are all artificial; but that – that would be cheating!"

"Oh, no," he said. "You see, 'aigrettes' are in fashion. The word 'real' has therefore become parliamentary. People don't want to be cruel, but they must have 'real aigrettes'. So, all these 'aigrettes' are 'real', unless the customer has a qualm, and then they are 'real imitation aigrettes'. We are a highly civilised people!"

"That is very clever," I said, "but how about the statistics of real egret plumes imported into this country?"

He answered like a flash: "Oh, those, of course, are only brought here to be exported again at once to countries where they do not mind confessing to cruelty; all, except – *those that aren't!*"

"Oh!" I said: "I see! You have been speaking ironically."

For Love of Beasts by John Galsworthy, 1912, RSPB Leaflet No 69.

2. Those formidable women

Galsworthy was just one of many eminent Victorians involved in the work of the Society whose positions of influence and powers of rhetoric made them potent allies. W H Hudson was another. Their polemics, many of them published under the Society's imprint, demonstrate the genius of the day for articulating moral indignation.

Hudson was particularly appalled by the practice of setting baited hooks, known as teagles, to catch birds as if they were fish. The victims were guaranteed to die in agony even if they managed to break free. Teagling was especially prevalent in the West Country, to which songbirds would flock when wintry weather gripped the South. The famished and exhausted birds would fall upon the bait; the countrymen would take only the larger specimens for food, throwing aside the others without bothering to put them out of their agony. The local ruling classes, increasingly unsure of their position, were reluctant, Hudson noted, to "denounce or interfere with these old pastimes or customs of the people".

There are so many varieties of suffering, so boundless is the ingenuity of evil, that the mind even of Man sometimes boggles when presented with a previously unworked vein of cruelty. What do you suppose the smallpox virus gets up to in the privacy of its own home, which is also, of course, our own body? If we had the eyes to see, and the capacity to interpret what we saw, would the havoc wrought among the corpuscles be recognisable as a form of behaviour on which we might be inclined to pass moral judgement?

Never mind: among the more subtle forms of cruelty that came of age during the 19th century was collecting, a harmless-enough pursuit in itself, one would have thought, and as natural to the species as passing water, falling in love, or committing homicide.

The female of the species, suitably bedecked, remember, in the plumage of lesser life-forms, was much given as ever to picking flowers. So assiduously did she pick, encouraged by her mate (it kept the little woman out of trouble, after all), which is to say, so voracious had the notorious national appetite for gardening become, and so rapacious the commercial interests which catered to it, that many areas of the countryside rapidly became denuded of most things worth picking in the first place.

It would be tedious to list the species involved. Few of us have ever seen them anyway, and most of us never will. The descendants of those that were tenacious enough to defy extinction are occasionally on view on motorway or railway verges, or at Marks & Spencer.

Birds, of course, as Galsworthy has already observed, were if anything even more attractive to collectors than plants. They were often just as colourful, if not more so, and they moved. If they sang as well, that was a bonus. Little birds in little cages for a shilling or less became a status symbol and a familiar sight, especially in London markets. W H Hudson in the RSPB leaflet *A Linnet for Sixpence*:

The Saturday evening market was in full progress at nine o'clock when I crossed the road on my way home. Just where I crossed, a crowd had gathered round a big man, standing by a barrow, who was bawling in a loud voice: and I stopped to look at him. He was a huge gross-looking man, with a broad, beardless, flabby face, and pale blue prominent eyes. He was holding forth to the people he had got together, trying in the street-seller's usual manner to keep their attention by his facetious oratory. "People wonder at me," he said, "because I'm so big. They keep on telling me I'm a stout man; and I grant you I do look stout among you Londoners. Now I'll tell you why I'm stout. I'm a Yorkshireman, and in Yorkshire we live on roast beef and Yorkshire pudding, and plenty of it; and bitter beer to drink; and don't you forget the plum-pudding! That's the fare to make a man stout! And I'll tell you another thing: I've been eighteen years in this business of selling linnets, and I've sold as many thousands in eighteen years as the oldest man in the trade in all his life. If you'll listen to me I'll tell you why, I've sold more because I give you a better bird – a cock linnet – a good strong bird, fresh caught, just up from the country, for sixpence. *Six pence* for a cock linnet worth half-a-crown. Can I say better than that?"

Here he thrust his hand into a box and pulled out a linnet, which he took by the legs and held up so as to make it flutter and beat with its wings before them all. After he had held it some time a sixpenny piece was handed up and the buyer received the bird and went his way. Then followed a few more words and another bird was produced and made to flutter, and eventually sold. Then another and another until a dozen or more had been disposed of while I stood looking on.

To what a place had the little flutterers been brought for sale – these little exiles in London town! And what a seller; and what buyers who would, in most cases, take them home to close, foul tenements. There must have been a hundred persons gathered round him, the pale, weary-faced, Saturday-night buyers from the mean streets. There they stood, silently gazing and listening in the glare of evil-smelling naphtha lamps, while the people who crowded the streets went jostling on either side, and the raw misty air was filled with the noise of scores of hawkers and stall-keepers all shouting their loudest.

A linnet – think of it! The small bird of our open spaces, which is, in its brilliant faculties, its delicate lovely spring colouring, and, above all, in its voice – those exquisite fairy notes, glad, yet tender, which it sings among the blossoming furze – the species which merits above all our feathered fellow creatures the epithet 'spirituel,' that Michelet applies to birds generally. And in its life, how beautiful the linnet is! Social above other kinds, there is always perfect harmony among the members. No bickerings, no jars, even in the love season, that time of greatest trial, when jealousy and rage, if a creature be capable of such emotions, are apt to show themselves. Nor when paired do they break up their little companies, but are near neighbours that call to one another, and meet and sing together a hundred times a day. Another engaging quality to be noted is the linnet's love of the open space and of nature's wildness. He will not endure the confinement of woods and copses, but must have the wide earth and wide sky around and above him, and the dark prickly furze bush for a home and castle.

This is the bird, the aërial little gladdener of our commons, heaths, and uncultivated grounds, which is most harried and tortured by us; for we are all, in a sense, responsible for what the bird-catchers and bird-dealers are permitted to do. It is captured in tens and in hundreds of thousands all over the country, and despatched in all haste to London and the great provincial towns. It must indeed be sent up quickly, since not less than sixty per cent of the birds are known to perish in captivity within a week of being taken. The dealer, on this account, is anxious to dispose of them as soon as possible; it often pays him better to sell them all out at once for sixpence each, or even less, than to keep them a week on the chance of getting two shillings or half-a-crown apiece for the survivors. It is a shocking waste of life; yet the birds that perish during the first few days of captivity represent but a part, probably less than half, of the entire waste. As a rule the bird-catchers send up only the cock birds, since linnets cannot be made to breed in captivity, and the females do not sing and are consequently of no value. What then becomes of these? Alas! their merciless captor does not release them, as fishermen put back the undersized fish they take into the sea. He kills them; he pulls their heads off as he takes them from the nets and throws the little fluttering bodies aside as so much carrion. But in some cases, bird-catchers have told me, the little headless bodies are taken home to be eaten in linnet pies.

I thought of these things – of the linnet free and the linnet captive in our hands in this Christian city, and, thinking of it still, was about to turn away when the big man pulled out a fresh bird, and pressing its little legs to make it flutter, held it high over his head and bawled out that it was the last of the lot. I waited to see it sold, who would give sixpence for it? No one seemed inclined, and so he pressed the little legs to waken it up once more; and it fluttered and gasped, and fluttered again, and yet again – a feathered 'Little Pilgrim' striving with all its little might to wrest itself free, to fly from such a frightful destiny in this lurid city of the under-world into which a strange chance had cast it.

Finally, to save it from further torture, I handed up a sixpence, and the little struggler was thrust into a paper bag and given into my possession. It will die to-night, I said, but in a cool quiet place it will perhaps pass from life less miserably than if I had left it. So I took it home, and in a large fireless room at the top of the house where I kept my book lumber, I took it from the bag, and out it fluttered and then hopped on to a pile of books and settled down to roost there. To my surprise it was not dead in the morning; it was lively and vigorous, terrified at my approach, and anxious to make its escape. I wish I had then followed my first intention of throwing open the window and letting it fly out, but it was a bitterly cold morning with a grey clammy mist over London, and what, in such a place in such conditions, would the poor little country bird do? No, it was better to keep him a day longer, and then take

The Croft, Didsbury, nr Manchester, first home of the Society for the Protection of Birds, founded by Mrs Robert W Williamson.

him out (to Richmond Park or some such open place) and release him where he would be able to find food and water, and recover his strength. Meanwhile, to save him from possible accident it was necessary to place him in confinement, and as there was no cage in the house I got an old wire screen which, set on a big tea-tray, made an airy commodious house for him. I put in a fern in a pot, the rim of which he subsequently used as a perch, and supplied him with food and water and left him by the open window. He was not wholly miserable there; on each of my numerous visits during that day and on the following day his terror appeared to diminish, and on my drawing back a little he would pick up the crumbs and other food I brought him, and he also appeared greatly interested in watching the sparrows that came for bread to the window ledge outside. I concluded that this linnet was one of the few that escape death during the first few days of captivity, and it seemed best not to set him free near London as I had resolved to do, but to keep him a couple of days longer, and take him to Worthing where I had arranged to spend the week end. There, close by, were the South Downs, which were perhaps his own home, and in any case it was the most suitable spot in which to restore him to freedom in the pure open world.

Having settled it in that way, I paid him my goodnight visit about eleven o'clock and found him at rest on his flower-pot, opening his bright eyes at the light; I then wished there had been some passage between us – some means of communicating the glad tidings of his approaching liberation, so that these last hours of his imprisonment might be lightened. But passage there was none; and in the morning I found him dead and cold, at the foot of his perch, under the fern.

Poor little brown bird in his modest winter dress, which would never now be changed for that brighter spring plumage his fellows would get in another month – the chestnut mantle and brilliant carmine vest. I had counted at first on his dying, but he had lived longer than is usually the case, and the wish had come, and with it the hope, to give him back to nature. Arrived at Worthing, my thought was, I would go out at once by Broadwater to the Downs and to Cissbury Hill, and on those long gorse-grown slopes that look towards the sea I would perhaps find a flock of wild linnets. The first sound of their tender airy twittering would reach him in his little cardboard prison and make him mad with desire to escape and be with them. That would be the moment to set him free; then how delightful it would be to watch his flight, so see him among his own little social people once more, free to use his wings under that wide sky.

This pleasure being denied me, there was nothing left for me to do but to put the little dead bird in a small box to take it with me on my trip to the coast; for it seemed to me that there would be a sort of satisfaction in giving the poor remains back to the green fresh earth.

It was a brilliant though very cold day in February when I walked out to Cissbury Hill; but though so early in the year a good many furze-bushes were already in bloom on the long southern slopes. Finding a suitable spot I made an excavation under one of the bushes and buried my linnet among its old red roots along with a wisp of green moss and a handful of furze blossoms.

And so ends the sad little story of the only linnet I have ever owned in my life, which I bought for sixpence.

A Linnet for Sixpence by W H Hudson, 1904, RSPB Leaflet No 50.

For love of birds: the story of the RSPB

Even the increasingly numerous natural history societies often served as cover for collectors, whose kleptomaniacal passion could ravish regional populations, especially of rarer species, which were of course the most sought after. Other species became rare simply because they were over-collected: the Dartford warbler is one classic case, and as recently as 1937 a Kite Preservation Fund, the last in a long series, was launched in an attempt to enlist the aid of farmers, traditionally the arch persecutors of birds of prey, in the battle against the armies of collectors.

If birds and their eggs tempted those collectors, so did insects, on which so many bird species, given half a chance, are wont to feed. And the plant collecting restricted the habitats available to those insects and, consequently or independently, to the birds themselves. The permutations are infinite, and only in recent years are they beginning to be understood by the various organisations, the Society included, whose initial preoccupations might have focused on one end or another of the food chain, or on one family or another in the kingdom of life.

Sophisticated though our understanding of the ecological web may have become, however, it is not always easy to understand the British obsession with birds: whether killing them, wearing them, collecting them or protecting them. In the development of, say, the Royal Society for the Prevention of Cruelty to Animals (which pre-dated the RSPB by more than half a century and which had been granted its Royal Charter by 1840) there is no obscure historical dialectic at work. Nor is the creation of a separate society for birds puzzling in itself – nor for butterflies, hedgehogs, pit ponies, dogs and cats – anything that moves, really, and many that don't.

But how has the RSPB become so big? What explains its presence in British life? Whatever the virtues of its leadership, however illustrious some of its membership, that in itself is not enough to account for such survival value.

Yet another of the Society's pamphleteers, the prolific W E Collinge, wrote in 1927 on the "national importance of wild birds". Noting that 100,000 song thrushes could be relied upon to devour more than three billion insects during the months of April, May and June each year, Dr Collinge nevertheless felt obliged to address himself to "another side to the subject of their national importance of equal interest, *viz.*, the aesthetic side".

He continued:

> "The beauty of and interest in wild birds has become interwoven into the life of all civilised nations; their song 'sweeter than instrument of man e'er caught' and their 'habitations the tree-tops are half-way houses on the road to heaven' – at least, Longfellow thought so, and so do tens of thousands of others. As a highly beneficial and important natural force aiding in the destruction of injurious insects and various injurious rodents, as objects of beauty conducive to the uplifting and welfare of mankind, we surely have a right to ask that the state will take all effective steps to guard and conserve such objects. If such action is withheld, neglected or not rightly applied, then the state has failed in its duty, and in consequence its subjects are bound to suffer, and its apathetic omission will call forth the condemnation of all far-sighted citizens.

> Think of your woods and orchards without birds!
> Of empty nests that cling to boughs and beams,
> As in an idiot's brain remembered words
> Hang empty mid the cobwebs of his dreams!
> Will bleat of flocks or bellowing of herds
> Make up for the lost music when your teams
> Drag home the stingy harvest, and no more
> The feathered gleaners follow in your door?''

That is probably as lyrical a description as one might wish of the British obsession with birds; but it is scarcely an explanation. Perhaps there is no explanation: it is a chicken-and-egg question, with the RSPB, appropriately, standing on both sides.

On the other hand (the history of the Society, as of the species, is rich in paradox), there is no gainsaying the force of *The Times'* assertion in 1870 that "many a man would shoot a bird without a pang who would hesitate to draw a trigger on a quadruped". E S Turner, who is perhaps best remembered as the author of *What the Butler Saw*, noted in his classic history of animal rights sentiment and legislation, *All Heaven in a Rage*: "This is still substantially true; in general, pangs only begin to be felt as the size of the quarry increases."

Even less obvious reason, then, for the supremacy of birds in the pantheon of British natural history. Except, perhaps, for this: in a small, ancient, densely populated, industrialised and still industrialising island nation, where was the competition? By the time we British had begun to consider the damage and suffering we had become wont to inflict on 'brute creation', birds were about all that remained of an indigenous fauna that in any case had been comparatively impoverished since the Ice Age and would have been even poorer were it not for introduced or naturalised species. The likeliest reason for the popularity of birds may well be the most blindingly obvious: unlike most wild mammals, extant or extinct, most wild birds can be seen during the day. There were household pets, of course; agricultural stock (although the decimation of what was once a dazzling spectrum of weird, wonderful and inimitably useful breeds was already well underway) . . . but otherwise the only remaining objects of affection for the determined cuddly-animal lover were rodents of one species or another, foxes, badgers, and, in increasingly remoter parts, deer.

The development of a national obsession with foxes or badgers might have had some interesting ramifications: there are those who would argue that the British national character in any case is most notable for its broad strains of distinctly fox-like cunning and brockish tenacity. But this was not to be. The badger was for far too long treated as vermin (as indeed were many bird species); the fox remains unprotected. Perhaps for that reason alone, perhaps by sheer bad luck, they failed to attract the legions of inspired amateurs, let alone the dedicated professionals, that have gradually turned us into a nation of bird-lovers.

For love of birds: the story of the RSPB

Sandwichboard men employed by the Society to patrol London West End streets, 10-29 July 1911.

We used to watch them every evening, the fair white herons in an irregular scalene triangle, winging their way down the great river to the lofty trees behind the colossal gilded Buddha, amid whose branches they roosted. Before that colossal Buddha every upcoming junk tied up to the shore, and captain and crew climbed the long straight flight of steps, then knelt and burnt at least one fragrant incense stick in gratitude for safe deliverance from half sunk jagged rock and frothing rapid. In contemplation of the many dangers by which we are surrounded in a state of nature, it is impossible for any man to believe that he delivers himself therefrom by his own skill; thus naturally the heart wells out with love and thankfulness to One wiser and more powerful, Who has guided his steps. And the outcome is an anthropomorphic or Pantheistic worship – fresh flowers with the dew upon them in Ceylon, lighted candles and tall white lilies in the south of Europe, crackers and burnt incense sticks in China. In the leafy sanctuary behind the

18

Fashion drawing of a lady's hat c 1900–1919. The caption read "The Mode of the Moment. A Charming Hat in Black and Grey. This very becoming hat is of black taffeta, underlined with black pedal straw and trimmed with oyster-grey and black brush ospreys."
"Ospreys" was the millinery term for the breeding plumes of egrets.

19

protecting image – for it was certainly thanks to the Buddha the trees had been spared to reach maturity – the birds slept safely, and each day we watched them homing and thereby knew the hour of the evening.

Day after day that flight of the herons would be an excuse for half an hour's idleness – *il giuoco degli occhi*, as the Italians call it. And after it we would go back to our books or writing, thankful for the interlude to the innocent white birds, whom we knew so well at nearer view, with their slight, elegant legs and graceful forms, the last finishing touch to so many a peaceful landscape.

Once we did a thing unheard of – accepted an invitation to stay a few nights in a grand Chinese country house, and travelled a day's journey in sedan chairs to arrive there. We had barely started on our return journey when my husband exclaimed, "By George, there they are!" The birds were accustomed to the trees, and always lived there all the year round. Now at this season of the year the rice where we then were was just the right cover for the insects that formed their food; at another season of the year it would be another place. The birds knew where to find their food at all the different seasons in the great circle, over which they could fly easily, of about twenty miles – as herons fly – from their home, the sacred grove. And in all their flights to and fro no man harmed them. Herons are got good for food, but they are what the Chinese call good to see. So the blue-gowned peasants looked at them, and talked of them in that soft Chinese that country people use of anything they love much, such as *Tu-ti*, the tutelary Deity of heaven and earth, or *Di-di*, baby, or the like. Painters painted them, from memory mostly, but their memories are good; poets used them for their similes. And no man nor boy in China harmed the herons.

But to make a sad story short. Bewick says the pretty creatures had been well-nigh exterminated in England even in his day, and since then the supply of egrets' crests has well-nigh given out in South America, whilst the demand for aigrettes is greater than ever; so one day my husband received a letter from an unknown correspondent offering him good terms for herons' crests from Western China. "Never!" my husband said, "never! Extirpate those beautiful birds here, as they have been extirpated everywhere else? No!" "Some one else will be sure to do it if you don't," said she who ought to have been his spiritual upholder. "I don't care. I won't." We came away and returned once again to Chungking, and there were the herons still. We greeted them with effusion, and once more knew the hour of the evening by the homing of the birds.

Then a telegram, and a half circling of the world, and the joys of London once again, mind rubbing against mind as a cow rubs its back against a tree-trunk, getting ease and refreshment thereby. Till one day came a box, a little box, sent by post, and inside it – such a little box – fifty pounds' worth of herons' crests. For the representative left in charge of my husband's business had had the same offer, and had accepted it all in the way of business. The transaction paid, of course, and people in London can nid-nod now at one another with the crests from Chinese egrets. But we know that when we go back to our Central Asian home there will be no beautiful white birds winging homewards to their nests above the Buddha, no homing of the herons to tell the hour of the evening; for those innocent white birds the people of China had spared for generations have, like so many others, been offered up as martyrs to the Moloch of European fashion. Doubtless the aigrettes' wearers have each their pets, are many of them perchance members of the Kennel Club, but those white birds were our pets. And we know that we shall see them never more, those herons we have watched so often in the long, long evening hours of life inside a Chinese city's walls.

Do our soldiers fight the better for their busbies made of egrets' crests? Would our lovely ladies not look ever fair if no plumes waved upon their heads?

Our Pet Herons, by Mrs Archibald Little, illustrated, 1900, Leaflet No 35.

It was the RSPCA that did the groundwork, that first fought the good fight in a spirit of rumbustious evangelism verging on the paramilitary, irresistibly reminiscent of the Salvation Army. Even today, the lads and lassies in their neat little uniforms, with their apple-cheeked rude health and their pathetically low salaries, seem likely as not to burst into Onward Christian Soldiers at the drop of a bonnet. As the brave inspector faces up to yet another stomach-churning case, armed only with moral indignation and a notepad (for remember, the RSPCA has no right in law to enter premises or to engage anyone in conversation if they are reluctant to talk), somewhere in the middle distance a celestial brass band oompahs along towards its supernal reward.

When it opened for business in 1824, the RSPCA, true to the dictum of *The Times*, concentrated on the larger quadrupeds: horses and cattle, primarily, and their ordeals in the marketplace. But its members learned fast. Bear-baiting and cock-fighting followed, and by the middle of the nineteenth century wild birds had come to number among its preoccupations, with the Sea Birds Preservation Act of 1869 among its most impressive monuments.

Arguably, the RSPCA set the tone, with its faults as well as its virtues, its amateurism and its professionalism, its idealism and its ruthlessness, for the whole of the nature conservation and animal rights movement in Britain. Certainly the RSPB would never have existed in its present form without it; in fact, the Society as such first met in the offices of these venerable pioneers.

The Selborne Society for the Protection of Birds, Plants and Pleasant Places was founded in 1885, invoking the shade of Gilbert White in its determination to widen the concerns of the anti-cruelty movement. Its purpose was initially fourfold: "To preserve from unnecessary destruction such wild birds, animals, and plants, as are harmless, beautiful, or rare; to discourage the wearing and use for ornament of birds and their plumage, except when the birds are killed for food or reared for their plumage; to protect places and objects of interest or natural beauty from ill-treatment or destruction; to promote the study of natural history."

Whatever the achievements of its predecessors, the vision of the Selborne Society for the Protection of Birds, Plants and Pleasant Places was breath-takingly ahead of its time. It would be some decades before most British practitioners of the art of conservation could accommodate their variously parochial notions of environment to an approach that was as sophisticated as it was generous.

Turner notes the catholic interests of "the true Selborne Society member", quoting from the first issue of its *Nature Notes* a description of one

"who loves every stone of the old abbey, beautiful even in its ruins, and

21

Winifred, Duchess of Portland, 1863-1954

The lives of the privileged seldom make very exciting reading. They are born into comfortable circumstances, they live easily and on the whole rather less traumatically than the rest of us, and they tend to die, logically enough, as rich in years as in material wealth or establishment honours. They do not have to try terribly hard, as we do, simply to keep going. Above all, they have the ultimate luxury, time. If excitement is what you want, look for war, look for poverty, hunger, disease, addled sexuality and early death. That is why we know so much about those among the well born who have managed, probably out of boredom as much as anything, to complicate their lives in some appalling way: the homosexuals, traitors and other degenerates, the adventurers, the monsters; and those who have managed to become embroiled in the more apocalyptic events of their time, that is to say, in real life. And occasionally, the artists, whose natural gifts – if you are not of the school which believes that conflict and despair are the true progenitors of creativity – are that much more likely to be recognised, nurtured, developed as their families are not preoccupied with hunger, warmth, shelter and other such exigencies of animal existence.

We are always pathetically grateful to such people when they manage not to make us feel quite as uncomfortable as they might. The most honorable epitaph, as far as we less favoured mortals are concerned, is: "He/she was not a bully." By all accounts Winifred, the Dowager Duchess of Portland, DBE, was not a bully. She was also not at all bad looking, and seems to have worked hard, by the standards of her class and era, to do the good that was expected of her.

She died, aged 91, in 1954, after 65 years as President of the Society. At that time "Her Grace", as the obituary in *Bird Notes* observed plaintively, "was the first and only President the Society has ever had." She had also, as it happened, been vice-president of the RSPCA. During the earliest days of the campaign against the plumage trade, she had, "by herself wearing hats trimmed only with feathers taken from the domestic fowls of Welbeck, showed that in the matter of personal adornment, such feathers could be just as becoming as those from the osprey or bird of paradise, without any question of despoilation or suffering being involved".

The Times described her as "that rarest of characters, a woman who spent more than half a century amid great possessions in the company of kings, queens and statesmen, but who was totally unaffected by her background and was capable of winning the friendship and trust of the most modest men and women with whom she found a common interest . . . an outstanding woman: and there are many to grieve at her passing".

Let us not forget that a bird is a bird is a bird. I suspect it is for her work among the miners of Nottinghamshire, whose petition in 1935 on behalf of "that angel, our beloved Duchess" led to her being created DBE (can anyone reading this book even begin to imagine what it must have been like to be a miner in Nottinghamshire in 1935?), that she will be remembered. People matter more than birds. Such is the cruelty of nature.

reverently garners the legends of its ancient fame, will strive also to preserve the trees and flowers that gather round its walls, and the birds that have in its desecrated altars 'a nest where they may lay their young'".

It was perhaps unfortunate for the development of the RSPB that it should have gone, initially at least, in a different direction from this group of visionaries, who by 1886 had established 11 branches, mostly in Hampshire and Surrey. That same year, Selborne merged with an eminent if loosely organised 'league' of anti-plumage campaigners that included John Ruskin. Centred on the home of Lord and Lady Mount-Temple at Broadlands, Hampshire, the Anti-Plumage League was an early example of how, in the words of Dr Robin Doughty, who has written the definitive study of the plumage trade, "a number of English aristocrats, out of the pages of Debrett, closed ranks behind moves in the 1880's to discourage the use of ornamental plumes".

By the time the RSPB received its Royal Charter in 1904, in addition to the Duchess of Portland, who was the Society's President, it could number among its vice-presidents no fewer than two duchesses, a duke, four earls, a countess, a marquis, a marchioness, a viscount and two bishops. But curiously enough, the Society had emerged in the first place because even so illustrious a marriage as that between the Selborne and Anti-Plumage groups had failed to answer the swelling public – or at least establishment – demand for curtailment of the plumage trade.

It was probably the very breadth of the Selborne vision that undid it. Notwithstanding its merger with the 'League', its members could never stomach the zealous and dogmatic approach, insisting that they saw no reason why the plumage of gamebirds and species deemed harmful to farmers should not be worn, as those creatures would be killed anyway. And even with those disclaimers, it was held to be contrary to the spirit of Selborne to require members to sign any kind of pledge renouncing or limiting the wearing of feathers. That was a serious tactical error. Professor Newton's dictum, as recalled by Turner, that "feathers on the outside of a biped called for the addition of tar", was the sort of thing that more and more people wanted to hear.

The original 'Society for the Protection of Birds' first saw the light of day, as an anti-plumage group, in Didsbury, Manchester, in February 1889. There is some confusion as to whether it was actually called the 'SPB', or anything at all, at that stage; but there is no doubt that, appropriately enough, it was women, led by Mrs Robert W Williamson who founded and ran it, and the influence of women (something of a stranglehold, as would be later deemed, when the inevitable waves of young Turks – male – crested and broke) was to persist.

Margaretta Louisa Smith, who as Mrs Frank E Lemon ran the Society from 1892 until the late 1930s, wrote of those early days:

> "The movement began in a small way, and for the first few months of its existence was confined to efforts to enlist the sympathy of women in support of protests against the wanton slaughter of birds for the sake of their plumage."

That first group of 'formidable women' (an epithet that turns up somewhere in virtually every mention of the early days of the Society) "had high hopes that by enrolling a sufficiently large number of women, the demand for ornamental plumage would cease and the supply would automatically come to an end. . . . these hopes were but short lived. The trade in birds' feathers throughout the world increased by leaps and bounds, and for every hundred women who eschewed the purchase and wearing of feathers, there were hundreds of thousands who would not listen and did not care".

It is enlightening to note how vigorous and persistent is the exploitative instinct in man (and woman) the destroyer. Notwithstanding the declared purpose of the Society, founded according to its first annual report in 1891

"in the hope of inducing a considerable number of women, of all ranks and ages, to unite in discouraging the enormous destruction of bird life exacted by milliners and others for purely decorative purposes",

and at least partly in reaction to the failure of similar groups to take a strong enough line on that issue, nevertheless, the Society's Rules stipulated merely that

"the Lady-Members shall refrain from wearing the feathers of any birds not killed for purposes of food, the Ostrich only excepted."

Such niceties could hardly survive the campaigning fervour necessary to achieve lift-off. They do suggest, however, not only a perhaps unexpected degree of hard-headedness among this inaugural cell of 'formidable women', but also a fundamental strain of pragmatism that was to serve the Society well in the century to come.

Mrs Lemon was a near neighbour of Mrs Edward Phillips who, from her home in Croydon, had begun to organise a series of 'Fur, Fin and Feather' afternoons, at which Hudson was among the more notable participants. On Sundays they would go to church and record the names of women who wore plumed hats; hectoring letters would follow on the Monday, denouncing "the cruelty of a practice which meant starvation and death for numberless orphaned fledglings . . .".

It was only a matter of time before two such like-minded groups discovered each other. The Manchester and Home Counties contingents merged in 1891; the former moved to London, where it met at first in Jermyn Street, at the RSPCA's headquarters. A formal constitution was drawn up (by Mr Lemon, who happened to be a solicitor), and Winifred Dallas-Yorke, Duchess of Portland, sowed the seed of eventual royal patronage with her election as president, which she was to remain for more than 60 years until her death in 1954.

W H Hudson took over from Mrs Phillips as Chairman of Committee in 1894; but this giant among naturalists, perhaps the most potent ally enlisted by the Society in its history to date, proved to be such a poor administrator that he stepped down (with a huge sigh of relief, presumably) in favour of Montagu Sharpe one year later.

With a membership fee of tuppence a year (a shilling for the branch secretary), and a far-sighted policy of decentralisation, all committed to the destruction of the plumage trade, the infant Society flourished. By 1898 there were 152 branches and 20,000 ordinary members; one of several overseas branches, in India, brought about the first anti-plumage legislation, a banning order in 1902 prohibiting the export of bird skins and feathers.

Throughout this early, heady period of expansion, and for many decades afterwards, the Society was to maintain its character – verging, indeed, on caricature – as the archetypal British voluntary organisation operating from a position of hereditary privilege, run mainly by and for women. Nicholas Hammond, a career executive with the RSPB and in many ways a good example, even today, of the manly side of the breed, has written of the Society in the thirties:

> ". . . the Society was an organisation run by elderly people. Many of them were those worthy pioneers who founded the Society in 1889. Their early contribution had been almost beyond praise: they, respectable ladies and gentlemen, had fought in the face of fashion to change public attitudes and the use of wild birds' feathers in hats.
>
> "Socially, the membership of the Society was well established as an upper middle class organisation with a sprinkling of aristocracy. Indeed, the Vice-Presidents' list read like a combination of Debrett, Crockford's and the more senior part of the Army List. The Council was scarcely less grand, which had been just as well in the early days when the Society needed influence if it was to achieve anything. . . ."

Change was in the wind by that time, of course; but it would still take until well into the fifties before the Society began to develop recognisably into the prosperous, professional – almost excessively smooth, its critics might argue – conservation machine we know today. One especially risible example of how far we, British society no less than the Society, have come in how short a time, is the fate of a little pamphlet printed in 1969 as a pocket history of the Society, and a very good one, too.

Titled, logically enough, *Protecting Britain's Birds*, and featuring on its cover an early photograph of the late Duchess of Portland, a beautiful woman presented in the fashion of the day as the most exquisite cameo, the pamphlet was never distributed – by some accounts because it was felt that the design was too old fashioned, and by other accounts because the juxtaposition of the photograph and the title line was considered unfortunate. It could hardly have helped that the author of the article on which the pamphlet was based, a Society librarian whose name was also prominently displayed, was Dorothy Rook.

In its text, that publication too notes the almost exclusively feminine composition of the early Society. The women, the author declares, "were attracted to it by the emotional appeal of the plight of young birds left to starve in the nest while their parents were shot down for their plumes". Debrett is invoked yet again, and the appropriate names dropped: the Baroness Burdett-Coutts; Margaret, Ranee of Sarawak; Sir Edward Grey (afterwards Lord Grey of Fallodon); Lord Lilford, and the Poet Laureate, Alfred Austin.

Voluntary organisations are no different from any other individual or group of individuals in the human or natural environment. Their fortunes wax and wane; there is a pattern to their histories of babyhood, youth, maturity, old age and death. They are literally 'organic', as the root of the word suggests. If such an organism survives (and

26

many do survive, of course, even if only to repeat the pattern all over again), it is inevitably in a form so changed from the original that it is clearly of another generation, as different from the parent body as son from father or grandfather, but with a family resemblance that remains nevertheless equally striking.

To this day, the congenital strain of *noblesse oblige* is perpetuated in the Society, as in so many others of its kind in this country; partly, of course, because of its Royal Charter, but also because the British tradition of amateurism has maintained a climate in which it thrives. It may co-exist with a membership approaching half a million, and a management structure as democratic (or not) as any other. But it persists as obviously as a nose, or a chin or an aptitude for music, or any other family trait.

What privilege means, after all, is that one has the time (because victory in the struggle for one's own survival has been signed, sealed and delivered at birth) for such relatively trivial matters as the preservation of birds. What it means at its best, is that one is also equipped, in terms of education, sensibility, and a position of influence in society, to bring something of value to the cause.

It should hardly surprise us, then, that as Dorothy Rook wrote in that ill-fated leaflet,

> "the Society seems to have found some of its staunchest adherents in the very kind of people who might have been expected to wear the fatal plumes".

Nor should the atmosphere generated by such people surprise us, even one hundred years later. Atmosphere is important; and, for a campaigning organisation, a tool like any other.

The cause itself generates an atmosphere, too. For example: on a visit to the headquarters of the United Nations Environment Programme in suburban Nairobi some years ago, I was struck most by the spectacle of massed bureaucrats in all their shapes, sizes and colours browsing in deep contentment all day long, or so it seemed, over coffee under the acacia trees. Among them was a small group of affable, mostly young, men with bemused expressions on their faces: the 'Outer Limits' team.

What joy, I thought, to spend one's paid time sitting around in an equatorial paradise pondering the hypothetical fate of the ozone layer, or the potentially damaging effects of fossil fuel burning on future generations of dugong. This, surely, was what environment was all about.

It may start with birds (or ozone or dugong) but it never ends there. I think that it is, in fact, the absence of 'limits', outer or inner, sensible or lunatic, that makes environmental concerns so addictive to those who study them. All human, animal and vegetable life are there; all habitats, circumstances, ecologies, processes and prospects; natural and unnatural, organic and inorganic; atomic, molecular, elemental . . . transcendent.

The great and good of Great Britain – the privileged, if you like – have always responded to this. In most recent memory, for example, it was a relative handful of members of the House of Lords who steered the monumental Wildlife & Countryside Act, tortuous jot by painstaking tittle, safely through an initially indifferent (if not downright hostile) Parliament. It was no accident. The Lords had the background, the resources and the inclination to create a piece of legislation that is no less a part of the British heritage than, say, London's Royal Parks, created for much the same reasons, by much the same sorts of people.

Among the subjects relegated to the 'Outer Limits' team, incidentally, those few years ago, was acid rain, now the subject of almost daily newspaper headlines: then in the early eighties still considered the legitimate concern only of those working at the lunatic fringe of science.

Some weeks ago, two ladies – one a friend of the writer's – strangers to each other, were travelling up to London in a first-class carriage, when a casual remark about the weather, or some such topic, led to a long conversation between them. This at length turned upon a subject in which, as subsequently appeared, both were deeply interested – namely, man's cruelty to animals, and the extermination, mainly for purposes of fashion, of so many beautiful and useful species of birds. One of the ladies spoke with such very great warmth on this subject, that the other, perhaps thinking the feeling displayed not altogether consistent, and inspired with a sudden boldness, remarked: "But, madam, you are yourself wearing an aigrette in your bonnet!"

"Yes, I know I am," she answered, surprised at the observation, and greatly wondering why it had been made.

The other, seeing how the case stood, explained. When the travellers parted at their journey's end, she who wore that graceful decoration – graceful and pleasant to see to those who do not know how it is obtained – declared that as soon as she reached her home she would remove it from her bonnet, and never wear, nor permit her daughters to wear, such an ornament again.

Judging from the numbers of aigrettes seen at the present time, it appears probable that there are very many among us who are as little acquainted with the ugly truth of the matter as was the lady in the railway carriage. At all events, one does not like to believe that any humane person, after learning the facts, *could* exhibit this kind of decoration with a light heart. Ladies have repeatedly assured me in all seriousness that milliners make these fine plumes out of the commonest white feathers. Others believe that they are the feathers of an Indian or some exotic bird called osprey, which is only another name for the ossifrage or sea-eagle. How the egret's delicate ornamental plumes first came to be called *osprey* in the trade I am unable to guess, unless it be because when arranged in an aigrette they form a *spray*.

Aigrette is French for egret, a kind of heron: aigrette, an ornament, originally meant simply a tuft of loose drooping plumes like the heron's crest. The word has somewhat changed its meaning with us: the aigrette worn by ladies in our day is in very nearly all cases actually made of the slender decomposed feathers that grow at one time of the year on the egret's back, and drop gracefully over the sides and tail of the bird. The less fine plumes, with shorter and stiffer filaments, forming the yellow aigrette, are plucked from the buff-backed or squacco heron, which is not an egret.

Of egrets there are six or seven species, or varieties, and they are found in all hot

28

and warm countries. One kind breeds in South-Eastern Europe, and even visits England occasionally. Another species ranges over India, China, Japan, and Australia; still others inhabit Africa and America. They are all true herons; patient catchers of fish, like that ghostly grey bird we are familiar with at home; with broad concave wings and a placid flight; cloud-seekers when pursued by a falcon; but they differ from other members of the same genus in their slighter build and more graceful lines, their snow-white plumage, and the nuptial ornaments of those fine decomposed feathers that ladies value so highly.

It is a very beautiful bird: all birds are in a measure beautiful, but they differ in beauty as one star differeth from another star in glory. When a small boy I was once greatly surprised to hear a gentleman talking about birds observe that, after having seen many very lovely kinds in tropical and temperate countries, he had come to the conclusion that the domestic pigeon was as much to be admired as any species. Its colouring was modest – harmonious blues and greys, touched with iridescence on the neck – but its lines were so perfect – it was so beautifully proportioned! Colour is very much more to the child's aesthetic sense than form or sculpture. At that early period my own belief was that the humming-bird exceeded all creatures in loveliness. Not dead in the hand, when it has only a scientific value and interest; nor a dead humming-bird worn in a lady's hat, which to my mind is a thing hateful to look at, as I fancy that it should be to every person who has a proper sense of the fitness of things. For it is the art of savages, who are without art, to decorate themselves with teeth and shells and feathers. But a humming-bird living, balanced motionless in mid-air, or dancing its marvellous aërial dance in the brilliant sunshine. It is indescribable and unimaginable: an airy fairy bird-form, suspended not on wings, which are changed by swift vibratory motion to a semicircle of mist, and exhibiting as it pauses and turns itself this way and that, colours as changeable and more splendid than those on a soap-bubble; and in a moment, even while you look, lo, it has vanished, as if it had been a fairy indeed, or a mere brilliant phantom of the mind, so swift is its passage through the air!

I wonder if any lady who had once seen this vivid little creature alive and sparkling among the flowers *could* wear it as an ornament – dead and dusty and crushed out of shape, all its glory gone! I wonder if its small red heart – round and ruby-red, like a small ruby worn on a finger-ring – a little while ago swiftly pulsating with the intense joyous energy of life, were to be placed in any lady's palm—— But this is to digress.

Among the birds that excel in magnificence of colour, others might mention the trogons, toucans, jacamars, some kingfishers, and some of the yellow and green and purple fruit pigeons of the East; parrots, tanagers, orioles, honey-suckers; gold and silver pheasants; the peacock; the impeyan pheasant; the resplendent and sacred quetzal, and the crested orange and scarlet cock-of-the-rock. Those who, like Wallace, have observed the birds of paradise disporting themselves in their native haunts, exhibiting their wonderful feather ornaments, regard these birds as surpassing all others in loveliness. Ruskin tells us that the familiar swan is the most beautiful bird: that is, when viewed resting peacefully on the surface of a stream, or to quote George Moore's description, slowly "propelling its freshness to and fro, balancing itself in the current," its bosom deep in the darkening water in which the white form is imaged, the long proud neck curved, and the broad arch of its ruffled

Mrs Lemon, 1860-1953

They most certainly were a band of 'formidable women', who in different times would have given suck to giants. Perhaps they did, but their offspring are unknown to us because they have had the good sense to keep out of the public eye and devote their lives wholeheartedly to selfish pursuits, in which case I have no doubt they have been prodigiously successful.

What is also beyond doubt is that if any one person can take credit for creating the Society it is Mrs Lemon. In that sense, she did indeed bequeath a giant to the world. Like the Duchess of Portland, Mrs Lemon lived to a ripe old age, 93 to be exact, and died within a year of Her Grace, in 1953. Also in common with the Duchess, Mrs Lemon seems to have been totally indefatigable, with that remarkable if paradoxical capacity for singlemindedness in all directions which brings results. In addition to her work for the Society she was a VAD Commandant during the First World War and in charge of Redhill War Hospital; other good works devolved upon the Royal Earlswood Institution and Crescent House Convalescent Home, Brighton.

Her obituary in *Bird Notes* opines: "Without Mrs Lemon there would have been no RSPB." Her obsession with birds is said to have begun when as a young girl she read

"Mrs Brightwen's book *Wild Things Won by Kindness*" and "began to think seriously about the treatment of birds, and her indignation at the slaughter of birds during the mating season for the sake of the plumage was fully aroused".

They may not make them quite like Mrs Lemon any more, but the type is not totally unknown to later generations. Even at this far remove, she strikes me as one of those whose Christian name was once and forever 'Mrs', if you see what I mean, and the "fully aroused indignation" of such a one must have been a minor miracle of energy. Her official Christian names were in fact Margaretta Louisa.

We know that she had a ready wit and strong sense of humour because her obituary tells us so. There seems to be little archival evidence of those things, but what does come through clearly is the "strength of character and tenacity of purpose". This made her a difficult character, "a woman of strong prejudices (as she herself would have been the first to admit)" who "set a very high value on personal relationships" . . . all of which was to surface apocalyptically when the inevitable bust-up came.

"To the office staff she was something of a dragon at times, but no one in trouble ever appealed for her help in vain, when all the forces at her command were called into play." That is probably the nicest thing you can say about a 'dragon', perhaps about anybody. The shadowy but diligent Mr Lemon (I think of him as 'Frank') must have been a perfect complement to his wife: the nice policeman, the easy-going administrator, to the Fulminator in Chief. Frank E Lemon was a lawyer, and every Society needs one of those.

Wouldn't it have been glorious to have been, just for a few short moments, a fly on their bedroom wall?

pinions seen against the luminous crimson disc of the setting sun.

Here we are let into the secret of the matter. There is the emotion caused in us by entire visible nature, and the emotion received from the contemplation of any single beautiful object in nature; and the two may strike the heart together, or correspond in time, and become one. Furthermore, just as nature as a whole has 'special moments' that have 'special grace', so it is with bird life; and with the individual bird, if seen at its best in certain conditions and in harmony with its surroundings, then, whether it be the jaçaná, or hoopoe, or sun-bittern vibrating its strangely-painted wings, as if in pure delight at their quaint loveliness; or the lyre-bird exhibiting its tail, or the argus-pheasant its ocellated plumes; or the ibis, or crane, or flamingo in statuesque attitude; or the floating swan, as Ruskin saw it, glorified by the setting sun; or any one of a hundred or of a thousand species, that particular one will strike the beholder as the most perfect – as possessing a charm above the others, and as the living central gem of which all visible nature forms for the moment only the appropriate setting.

I have at times had this feeling about some herons. It may be only a fancy of mine, but it strikes me as not improbable that when the ancient Egyptians selected the *bennû* – which we know from their representations to have been a heron, most probably the crested purple species – as a symbol of the sun, and called it 'the soul of Ra', and 'the heart of the renewed sun', they were accustomed to regard this bird as one rich beyond others in beauty.

A South American species which I have always greatly admired is the *Ardea sibilatrix*, prettily called by the Guarani Indians, on account of its melodious cry, *Curahí-remimbí*, or *flute of the sun*. It has white eyes and green legs and beak; its loose plumage, which is soft as an owl's, has two colours, clear grey and pure pale yellow, harmoniously disposed.

At other times it has seemed to me that the egret is the most lovely bird of this special type. Its entire plumage is of a whiteness surpassing that of other kinds, so that when viewed side by side with it, the swan and wood-ibis and stork look dull and earthy by comparison. In allusion to this excessive whiteness, different species have received the scientific names of alba, immaculata, candidissima; but no words can give an idea of how white the egret really is. It is as if the bird had some luminous quality existing within itself, which shows through the plumage, and gives it among birds something of a supernatural appearance. The egret is seen at its best standing motionless on some dark dead branch, or on the margin of the water against the deep greens and browns of aquatic foliage, the neck curved to the form of an S, the golden dagger beak inclining downward at a slight angle, and the plumage showing white as a drift of lately fallen snow with the clear sunshine glinting on it – a bird-statuette carved by some divinely-inspired artist out of a white crystalline stone found in no earthly quarry.

This is the bird which is sought after in its haunts and killed for the sake of its few ornamental feathers. These feathers, as I have said, are nuptial ornaments, found in both sexes, and appear only in the love season: consequently, to get them, the bird must be slain when pairing or about to pair, or when breeding; but those who engage in this business know that to obtain a good supply with little trouble, the birds must be taken when the breeding season is well advanced. During the greater part of the year the egrets live singly, in pairs, and in small flocks; but when nesting they form communities, like rooks and gulls, and our own heron. The egret's heronries are formed on low trees or bushes, or on reeds growing in the water, and the nests, sometimes to the number of three or four hundred, are placed close together. The feather-hunters consider it a rare piece of good fortune when they discover one of these breeding places, when the birds that at other seasons live scattered over a wide expanse of country are found massed together. The best time to attack them is when the young birds are fully fledged, but not yet able to fly; for at that time the solicitude of the parent birds is greatest, and, forgetful of their own danger, they are most readily made victims. I have seen how they act when the heronry is approached by a man; they take wing and hover in a cloud over his head, their boldness, broad wings, and slow flight making it as easy as possible to shoot them down; and when the killing is finished, and the few handfuls of coveted feathers have been plucked out, the slaughtered birds are left in a white heap to fester in the sun and wind in sight of their orphaned young, that cry for food and are not fed.

There is nothing in the whole earth so pitiable as this – so pitiable and so shameful – that for such a purpose human cunning should take advantage of that feeling and instinct, which we regard as so noble in our own species, and as something sacred – the tender passion of the parent for its offspring, which causes it to neglect its own safety, and to perish miserably, a sacrifice to its love! It is an outrage on Nature, a crime more detestable and abhorrent to our sense of justice, and to every kindly feeling in us than crimes innumerable which men are driven every day to commit by evil associations, by want, by drink, by insanity, and for which they are hunted down, and condemned to long terms of imprisonment. And those who, not ignorant of the facts, encourage such things for fashion's sake, and for the gratification of a miserable vanity, have a part in it, and are perhaps more guilty than the wretches who are paid to do the rough work.

It is not only the beautiful white egret: there are scores and hundreds of the loveliest known species of birds that are in the same case. A nuptial dress is well-nigh universal in this class of creatures. We see here that there is a close and curious analogy between birds and plants that have a blossoming and seed time. The season in plants, when they take on the glory of flowers, corresponds to the love season in bird life – there is perfume in one and melody in the other; and in cases where the bird acquires a new and brighter plumage and feather ornaments, as in the egrets, these deteriorate and drop off at the end of the breeding season, just as petals wither and fall when the flower is set. It is when in that gayer dress that birds are most valuable for the purposes of fashion and for other forms of decoration; nor is this all; it is then that they are most easily found and taken. The shyest, most secretive kinds lose all their wild instincts in the over-mastering anxiety for the safety of eggs or young. And when the poor bird, uttering piercing cries, its sensitive frame quivering, its bill gaping as if the air could no longer sustain it in such intense agitation, and fluttering its lovely wings to make them more conspicuous, and by such means draw the danger away from its treasures and on to itself – when it has been ruthlessly shot for the sake of its feathers, its fledglings are left to starve in the nest. And if to the starved young we add all the birds that fly away with pellets of lead in their bodies to languish and die of their wounds, and those that drop down in dark forests, amidst the tangled undergrowth, and in dense reed-beds, and are never recovered, it would be no exaggeration to say that for every bird worn in a lady's hat, at least ten have suffered the death pang.

The effect of the millions of individual acts of cruelty of this description, which are annually inflicted on birds, is that a vast number of beautiful species, including all those that give the greatest lustre to bird life, are rapidly decreasing; and if the persecution continues, they must become extinct at no distant date. It could not be otherwise, since, as we know very well, the increase which takes place each year in any species at the breeding season is, in most cases, just sufficient to balance the annual losses from all natural causes. For this new artificial destruction, caused by a barbarous fashion and by powder and shot, Nature has made no provision.

I frequently hear it said that, with few exceptions, women care nothing for these things; that they are perfectly callous to the sufferings inflicted on the lower animals, and to their destruction, so long as sufferings and destruction are made in any way to conduce to their own pleasure; that they look on at the efforts now being made by the Society for the Protection of Birds, the Selborne and kindred Associations, and by individuals, with an amused curiosity, and nothing more; that if they have any pity for the persecuted creatures, any regret for the great harm being done, it may all be expressed in the words lately used by a lady contributor to one of our great fashionable weeklies:—"Poor dear little dicky birds! It is such a pity to kill them; but it is the fashion to wear them on our hats, and we cannot do without them."

I do not believe all this.

Cynical cruelty, real or affected, is hateful enough in a man; in a woman it is unnatural, and I do not for a moment believe that this lady speaks for any one but herself. I am acquainted with several ladies who have worn birds in their hats for years, who wear them no longer, whatever the fashion may be, and who grieve when they remember how, sinning from want of thought, they once used such ornaments. And as it has been with these, so would it be with others, with thousands and tens of thousands, if the facts could by any means be clearly brought to their knowledge, if they could be brought to reflect on the character and the disasterous consequences of this war against Nature, which is being waged at their behest for so unworthy a motive.

OSPREY, or, Egrets and Aigrettes, by W H Hudson, 1891, inc postscript 1 August, 1896. Leaflet No 3.

*Bird of Paradise –
RSPB Leaflet No 20.*

3. Featherheads

One of the many intriguing aspects of this chronicle is the way in which it brings together so many of the more inglorious activities of the human species.

On the one hand we have the ancient and, as many still consider it, honourable pursuit of birds as game, whether for eating or for sport shooting, with all the colourful and convivial traditions attached to it. Some call it bloodlust, and dismiss it; but as the manifold varieties of cruelty go, there is something to be said for controlled shooting. It is, or can be relatively speaking, an amiable enough pastime. Where appropriate, it keeps bird populations from outstripping their habitats; it helps, indeed, to preserve habitats that might otherwise vanish. It distracts certain members of society who might otherwise turn even more of their energies to increasing their personal fortunes at the expense of their less favoured fellow citizens. It even furnishes gainful employment for some in that less favoured class.

Similar arguments might apply to the second strand that runs through the pre-history and early history of the Society: the use of birds for fashion. It is all a question of emphasis, and degree. The hardest lesson for idealists of any stripe – conservationists, Labour Party supporters, the Flat Earth Society, the lot – is that right or wrong, as matters of fact or of ethics, are of only limited significance in the struggle for whatever ideal it is we have decided to strive for. What will convince people to support our cause is simply what appeals to their self interest.

That, unhappily, means a system of rewards and punishments. Virtually any success effected by any voluntary pressure group (a mutation in the social structure that the British, probably to their credit, insist on muddling up with the wholly unrelated convention of 'charity') is the result of hard-nosed campaigning, which, stripped of its rhetoric, comes down to a cunningly crafted series of threats, promises and more often than not a healthy dash of bribery.

People quite like the environment: cuddly animals, the countryside, the sea shore and Hovis commercials. But that does not mean, has never meant, that they would refrain from plundering or despoiling cuddly animals, the countryside, all the rest and each other, too, so long as it was in their apparent short-term interest – profit, amusement, expediency – to do so. What the conservationists had to do was to put together a system of reward and punishment, threats and promises, that would institutionalise and make respectable the only principles that really mattered even to their highest-minded supporters: the care, feeding and general all-round wellbeing of Number One.

What does Number One want? Whatever his position in society, Number One wants, initially at least, the same things as everyone else: employment, enough to eat, and sex. Among the many things he cannot be bothered about particularly (whatever he says) are world poverty, litter, and other people's children. Among the things he can be certain he does not want are nuclear power, foreigners and taxes. Among the things he will accept more or less meekly are war, bad catering, and prostitution.

Once his basic needs are, if not satisfied, then at least settled as far as they are likely to be in this life, Number One can turn his attention to a large subsidiary catalogue of luxuries and pleasures. Among those are innumerable ethical and aesthetic satisfactions that the higher-minded among us have for many centuries tried to define as imperatives. They are nothing of the sort; but they can come to loom large in the life of a Number One whose lot has improved sufficiently, or was never in need of improvement in the first place, or – an occasional but important possibility that British politicians are just beginning to take in – has reached a plateau of misery that is not quite dangerous to life but is so unlikely to improve that Number One has ultimately despaired and turned his mind to other things in order to obscure the dreadful consciousness of underprivilege and failure.

It is at this point that we are ready to pursue such agreeable amenities as a clear conscience or an appreciation, informed if possible, of books, music, art . . . or wildlife. Any voluntary body that seeks to increase its market share of Number One's preoccupations and priorities must first convince the public that the cause it is peddling has a direct bearing on real life – that is, preferably, self-preservation on the one hand, or comfort (call it morality, call it entertainment, it is nonetheless a mere gilding of the cage in which we must all try to survive) on the other.

As the campaign against the plumage trade intensified, women became increasingly ashamed of their millinery habits. But they carried on because the tyranny of fashion ranked higher in their self-centred scheme of things than the discomfiture engendered by the campaigners' ire. Social announcements in the newspapers – often, as Turner observes, the self-same newspapers, like *The Times*, that campaigned most strongly in their editorial columns against the plumage trade – continued to decree "wings will be worn". Women are like that, of course; so are men, so are newspapers.

There was a great deal of precedent to overcome. The Greeks and Romans hunted the ostrich for its plumes, and trade in peacocks is probably 5,000 years old. Pheasants were held to have been introduced to Europe by the Argonauts, while knowledge of the bird of paradise may pre-date Magellan. Heron and egret plumes are reliably reported to have been among the Crusaders' trophies.

Marie Antoinette was nicknamed 'Featherhead', and the doomed ladies of her court were not slow to emulate her passion for exotic plumes. Other European capitals followed suit. Reputations rose and fell with lugubrious regularity as ladies and their hairdressers strove to outdo each other. Some women had to kneel on the floor of their carriages or stick their heads out of the window as they travelled, in order to accommodate their grotesque coiffures. Courtesans moaned that the cost of keeping up with such absurd fashions was ruining them.

Anonymous satirists of the day lampooned these poor creatures – the women, not the birds – as

">... not content with looking like a jay,
But they must dress as lightly and as gay;
Nay, ev'ry tail, of ev'ry bird they rob,
And with the lightest feathers wing the nob;
Like horses move in the funereal train
Beneath their plumes, and shake the plaited mane.
Now, since to ornament the frolic fair,
There's not one pretty bird whose rump's not bare;
Do not the ladies more or less appear,
Just like the birds whose various plumes they wear?"

When the French revolutionaries started cutting off heads, the trimmings sloughed away with them. Austerity became the order of the day – but not for long. When the carnage began, there were no fewer than two dozen feather-dressers and plumage-mounters in Paris. Patience and longevity would have paid off here: Romanticism revived in relatively short order, and the Restoration of the French monarchy was crowned, inevitably, with bits and pieces of birds.

The United States was not immune to the contagion, of course; and the anti-plumage campaign has as interesting and honourable a story to tell on that side of the Atlantic as on this. As the market expanded, the fashion for plumage spread down the social scale, becoming perhaps a shade less grandiose than in the days of Louis XVI but far more sinister in the astronomical numbers of birds it consumed. There was not one decade of the last century during which birds did not figure prominently in European and American fashion, although the worst excesses developed from the fifties.

In *Feather Fashions and Bird Preservation*, Doughty recalls how

"in 1886, on two late afternoon excursions through uptown shopping areas of New York, Frank Chapman . . ., ornithologist and bird preservationist, noted that three-quarters of the 700 women's hats he counted displayed feathers.

"The feathers came from 40 different kinds of native birds, including sparrows, warblers and flycatchers . . . In Paris, at about the same time, dresses were edged with swallows' wings, downy tufts of marabou and flossy-smooth grebe skins. In London, one fashionable lady was observed in a gown hemmed with the heads of finches, and, unpardonable sin, the plumage of robin redbreast."

The numbers associated with this sort of thing, increasing regularly up to the First World War, verged on the incredible. According to Doughty, in the 50 years from 1870, 40 million pounds, or 20,000 tons, of ornamental plumage entered the United Kingdom each year, and that is disregarding that staple of the trade, ostrich plumes. Such figures "represent scores of millions of birds killed all over the world", Doughty notes. Table 1, reproduced from his book *Feather Fashions and Bird Preservation*, gives an idea of the extent of the trade.

For love of birds: the story of the RSPB

Table 1   Imports of Feathers into the United Kingdom

Decade	Types	Major source regions (in thousands of lb)		Total imports (in thousands)
1872-1880	Ornamental feathers and downs, including ostriches	Cape Colony farms India		2,444 lb 7,471 £
1881-1890	(as above)	Cape Colony (1885+ mainly ostrich India[a] France (1885+) Holland (1885+)	1,197 455 1,547 693	6,746 lb 13,837 £
1891-1900	(as above)	Cape Colony (mainly ostrich British E. Indies France Holland United States Latin America[b]	3,162 1,044 3,619 1,687 481 81	10,732 lb 11,692 £
1901-1910	(as above)	Cape Colony (mainly ostrich) British E. Indies France Holland[c] United States Egypt Venezuela	5,175 202 4,903 1,416 314 175 36	14,362 lb 19,923 £
1911-1920	(as above, excluding ostrich after 1912)	France	3,833	7,397 lb 9,376 £
1921-1930	Ornamental undressed feathers, excluding ostrich			193 lb 81 £

Source: UK, Board of Trade, *Statistical Abstract* 1876-1890 (London, 1891) and Customs Stat. Office, *Annual Statement of the Trade . . . with Foreign Countries . . .* (London, 1889, etc.).
[a] Figures incomplete after 1885, see P L Simmonds, *Journ. Soc. Arts* (1855), p. 849.
[b] Includes incomplete statistics from Brazil, Colombia, Venezuela and Argentina.
[c] 1906 statistics are inconsistent with imports from Germany suddenly increasing to over 250,000 lb annually, while others from Netherlands show dramatic declines.

The plumage industry was as truly an international phenomenon as any comparably massive enterprise based on commodities or manufactured goods today. Think of oil, electronics, pharmaceuticals; think of giant multi-national companies and their global reach. In the first decade of the new century, duty-free ornamental plumage imports into England were worth about £20 million.

Earlier, the Public Sale list of one London firm was thought likely to have contained more birds than the total of all the ornithological collections in the United States – more than 12,000 hummingbirds, 7-8,000 Indian and South American parrots, 1,000 woodpeckers, 5,000 tanagers, and so on and on – with a single dealer estimating that he had sold two million birds in a year.

Turner, as usual, rises to the occasion with the appropriate rhetorical flourish. He writes that by 1870,

> "At no time had birds been in greater need of protection. Never had they suffered such wanton abuse from the human race. Their foes were many and cunning: sportsmen, whether in the form of pot-hunting gentry, trap-pigeon shooters or the fast-multiplying race of 'cockney' sportsmen; gourmets, who could not look at a steak pudding unless it was preceded, or accompanied, by the tiny carcases of singing birds, which gave negligible nourishment to the already overfed; fashion designers, who ruled that women should clothe themselves in feathers; the plume and wing hunters, who recklessly supplied this demand; farmers, many of whom saw birds only as agents of depredation; dealers in cage birds; the tribe of netters, fowlers and trappers, who supplied birds for table, cage or sport; self-styled naturalists, who sought out rare birds and eggs; gamekeepers, who killed all birds which threatened the privileged creatures they reared for their masters to kill; schoolboys, who limed twigs, laid nets, robbed nests and stoned fledglings, or caught birds to sell to dealers who sold them to other schoolboys; and louts, who killed without a qualm anything that fluttered."

"At busy periods," he adds, "the dealers of London and Paris nearly suffocated under their wares." Hypocrisy (or, to be fair, blind inconsistency) was rife. Clergymen denounced the wearing of plumage from their pulpits, if they dared, over a sea of feathers. Those who were not so courageous trotted out the "His eye is on the sparrow" routine with little or no sense of incongruity.

From Florence Suckling's Humane Educator via Turner come these lines by the prolific Anon describing a woman hectoring a (male) shooter of grouse:

> She quoted Burns's "Wounded Hare",
> And certain stirring lines of Blake's
> And Ruskin on the fowls of air,
> And Coleridge on the water snakes.
> At Emerson's "Forbearance" he
> Began to feel his will benumbed,
> At Browning's "Donald" utterly
> His soul surrendered and succumbed.
>
> She smiled to find her point was gained,
> And went with happy parting words
> (He subsequently ascertained)
> To trim her hat with humming-birds.

For love of birds: the story of the RSPB

The RSPCA can take some of the credit for the first ever legislation aimed specifically at the protection of wild birds. The Sea Birds Preservation Act of 1869 and the subsequent Wild Birds Protection Act of 1880, were enacted well before the Society had come into existence, and although not terribly effective did establish a precedent to be exploited as time went on. Much of the public outcry that was ultimately to destroy the plumage trade focused on exotic species; but the timing of these first rudimentary acts of legislation reminds us that domestic bird populations suffered terribly in the cause of fashion, especially at the poorer end of the scale where the wings and feathers of gulls, starlings, even sparrows, enabled the humblest lady's-maid to emulate her mistress.

The explosion in the plumage trade, and the Society's efforts to beat down the conflagration, were the dramatic origins of a process that by its nature was bound to continue in a very much lower key. *Protecting Britain's Birds* takes up the story.

It is impossible to compare the membership figures of those early days with those of the present time because the entire organisation of the Society was so different. 'Members' were those who paid 2d for a membership card and signed a form pledging themselves not to wear the plumes of birds other than those of the ostrich. The last recorded figure for such 'members' was 22,000 in 1899. By that time there were also 'Associates' (who paid a minimum annual subscription of 1s) and Life Members who paid a guinea. The numbers of 'Associates' in 1899 was 3,856, making a grand total of 25,856. Although not comparable with the present-day figures, these are very interesting as showing what a tremendous interest there was in bird protection, triggered off no doubt by the emotional appeal of the protest against the plume trade.

The framing of a constitution in 1893 which fixed the subscription for Associates and Life Members was followed by the granting of a Royal Charter in 1904, and by that time we cease to hear of 'members', but there is no record of the date when the 2d membership card ceased.

Bird-catching was in the news in 1894. In 1897 the Society had a London address at 326 High Holborn, the office of that famous ornithologist, Harry Witherby, and of his firm, H. F. & G. Witherby, and at last a paid assistant secretary was appointed. It requires little imagination to appreciate the vast amount of voluntary work which must have gone into the growth of the Society.

In 1898 an appeal was sent to landowners to protect rare birds and to prohibit the use of the pole-trap. This diabolical instrument was actually made illegal in 1904. In 1898 the Society's Christmas cards were first published and 4,500 copies were sold that season. In 1899 the Queen confirmed an Order prohibiting the wearing of 'Osprey' plumes by the military. Royal interest in the abolition of the plume trade was further demonstrated in 1906 when Queen Alexandra wrote a letter to the Society for publication, expressing disapproval at the wearing of the plumes of breeding birds.

The first legacy (of £25) was received in 1900. In 1901 the first Watchers were appointed – to protect pintail at Loch Leven. The Society seems to have depended to a large extent on donations, and there are in the annual reports complaints about the disappointing result of the appeal for Watchers' Donations.

The 'Bird and Tree' Competition (in which W H Hudson took a great interest) was started in 1901 also. This was a competition for schools in which the children wrote essays describing a bird and tree which they had been studying, and the prizes were regional shields. The Society's journal, *Bird Notes and News*, was founded in 1903 which was also the year when the Society's bird postcards first appeared.

The year 1908 was an important one in the Society's history, because it saw the introduction to Parliament of the Importation of Plumage (Prohibition) Bill. The Bill, however, seems to have met opposition and the intervention of World War I finally put an end to all efforts to push it through. In that year also, as a result of the concern felt about the trade in caged birds, an Inspector was appointed by the Society to enquire into it.

It seems probable that the initial impetus which the Society had gained was by now dying down, and the annual report for 1911 showed only 127 new members and 34 new fellows. However, a new venture was started in 1913 when experimental perches were installed at two lighthouses (St Catherine's, Isle of Wight, and the Casquets) to help migrant birds which, dashing themselves against the lanterns, were being killed in thousands.

During World War I the plume trade seems to have become more or less dormant, presumably because of import restrictions. However, another cause for alarm was the appearance of song birds for sale in poulterers' shops – not because of the food shortage, but as a delicacy. This is an instance of the Society's continued vigilance where birds were concerned.

The annual report for 1917 showed only 102 new members, with the significant remark: "an increase on recent years". This was, however, a most important date for the plume trade, because a Board of Trade order came into force prohibiting the importation into the United Kingdom of 'osprey' plumes and other feathers obtained by the wholesale killing of breeding birds. This prohibition was followed by the Importation of Plumage (Prohibition) Act of 1921. This was virtually the end of the plume trade, and presumably milliners at last decided to bow to the inevitable, because there was a short note in *Bird Notes and News* in 1931 to the effect that there had been a revival in the wearing of ostrich plumes! The Society had thus at last attained the principal end for which it had been formed – but it had taken 32 years to do so.

Accounts of oil pollution were gradually taking the place of the plume trade in the annual reports and the journal, and great satisfaction was expressed when in 1925 a Preliminary International Conference on Oil Pollution was held in Washington. Great Britain had already taken the lead by the passing of the Oil in Navigable Waters Act, 1922, which prohibited the discharge or escape of oil into waters within the three-mile limit.

In 1928 toxic chemicals make their appearance as a menace to wildlife, with an article in *Bird Notes and News* calling attention to the danger to birds from the use of arsenical sprays in gardens, orchards and fields.

For love of birds: the story of the RSPB

Ever since 1901 the reports had contained a great deal of comment about watchers and bird sanctuaries, and in 1905 the first Watchers' Committee was formed. By 1914 there were ten districts under the care of this committee and 22 men employed to guard them. In 1930 it was announced that the Society had purchased some land at Cheyne Court in Romney Marsh as a bird reserve for wintering migrants. This land was eventually sold when agricultural drainage outside the sanctuary spoilt it for the purpose for which it had been acquired. In 1930 also, East Wood, Stalybridge, came into the Society's possession as a bequest, while 250 acres at Dengemarch in Kent were handed over as a gift.

The continuing sympathetic attitude of Royalty to bird protection was again instanced by an interesting little note in an issue of *Bird Notes and News* in 1930: "The action of HM The King in declining to accept the early plovers' eggs sent to him this spring has been received with general acclaim".

Pursuing its policy of energetically attacking the evil of oil pollution, the Society in 1931 prosecuted an oil company for allowing oil to escape from their vessel near Skokholm Island. The company was fined £25.

The propaganda against caged birds which the Society had pursued persistently by the issue of pamphlets, some of which were by W H Hudson, received its justification in 1933 when an Act was passed dealing with the traffic in British birds. This Act made it illegal to take, sell, offer for sale or have possession of for sale certain birds known to be normally taken for sale.

The Society now held the shooting rights of Brean Down in Somerset, the farmer from whom it obtained them being the voluntary watcher there. In 1935 Ramsey Island was purchased as a sanctuary with the co-operation of the Society which also took a ten years' lease of Llanddwyn in Anglesey. During 1937 there were 60 watchers who furnished reports of birds for their respective areas. Some were voluntary, some received small gratuities, and they were provided with uniform caps to wear. The RSPB's present Representative in Orkney received his first mention as assistant to the watcher in those islands. By then the Society owned 1,300 acres at Dungeness, 150 at Cheyne and five acres at Brean Down with a 99-year lease of the rest of the down. Brean Down, as well as Cheyne, had to be given up later as the encroachment of human habitation and invasion by trippers rendered it useless as a sanctuary. The Society held leases of other land in many parts of the country.

By 1939 the membership stood at 4,852 – and then came World War II. In 1940 the RSPB's London office received a direct hit, but it was a Sunday and the office was empty.

During the war all reserves except Bowling Alley Wood and Stalybridge were in the hands of the military. *Bird Notes and News* continued to appear throughout the war, but the membership dropped to 3,558 although the number of new members per annum increased. Indeed, birdwatching seems to have become more popular, probably as an antidote to the horrors of total war.

From the off, the Society always seems to have had an instinct for publicity, an instinct which has served it well to this day. Mrs Lemon notes that

"the Press extended a most encouraging welcome to the new Society, except, as was only natural, journals and newspapers devoted to trade interests; *Punch*

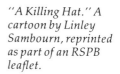

vigorously denounced the cruel fashion, and in May, 1892, published a striking cartoon by Linley Sambourne of a Harpy decked from head to foot in the spoils of birds slaughtered at the behest of fashion.''

The Times especially thundered away most creditably throughout the protracted struggle, and there seem to have been few weeks, right up until April Fool's Day 1922, when the Importation of Plumage (Prohibition) Act, 1921, came into force, that anti-plumage rhetoric failed to surface somewhere in its editorial or letters columns.

The involvement of eminent scientists in the crusade was an obvious advantage; but some of their more polemical flourishes in the scientific literature of the day would certainly raise eyebrows in this century, and probably did even then. In his *Dictionary of Birds* published in 1893-96, Newton, in a passage on Extermination, deplored "the rage for wearing . . . feathers, which now and again seizes civilised women who take their idea of dress from interested milliners of both sexes; persons who having laid in large stocks of what are known as plumes proceed to make a profit by declaring 'them to be in fashion'. The large supplies required by the plumage trade are obtained by laying waste the homes of birds during the nesting season.''

As men became increasingly drawn in to what had started out as a cadre of women, the Establishment cast of the Society if anything intensified. In 1893 Sir Herbert Maxwell of Monreith became a vice-president – and, as Mrs Lemon writes, ''the first among many Members of Parliament who warmly espoused the cause of Wild Birds, and supported in Parliament various measures introduced for their preservation and protection; a large proportion of these were directly instigated by the SPB which, in addition to drafting and getting Bills introduced, worked up public opinion in their favour outside as well as inside both Houses of Parliament, without which no Bill has much chance of reaching the Statute Book, or of subsequently being enforced''.

In the early years the Society was a rather peripatetic affair. From the establishment of the first London office in 1897, where the secretary and one paid assistant were given a room in the office of Witherby & Sons at 326 High Holborn, it was barely a year until the operation became too big, and several rooms were rented from the London Zoological Society at 3 Hanover Square. That house was demolished in 1909; the Society declined an offer from London Zoo to follow them to their new offices in Regent's Park, opting instead for proximity to Parliament from 23 Queen Anne's Gate and later 82 Victoria Street.

It was to be a very long time between the foundation of the Society and final victory in the struggle to suppress the plumage trade: roughly three decades, a generation as human lives are measured. By then, of course, there was far more on the agenda; for example, oil pollution was emerging as an issue, and appropriate legislation was passed (although enforcing it, and creating international machinery around it, was to remain a constant headache) as early as 1922, the same year in which the feather merchants' fate was sealed.

In the meantime, the Society distinguished itself in a curious campaign to find a means, as Mrs Lemon put it, ''for lessening the inevitable destruction during migration of birds at Lighthouses''. From 1913, devices, which she described as ''Bird Refuges or Perching Places'', were installed at Bardsey, Caskets, St Catherine's, Skerries, Spurn and S Bishop.

> ''By means of these huge perches, put up and dismantled for cleaning purposes'' – the mind boggles – ''before and after both the Spring and Autumn migrations, the lives of millions of birds have, since 1913, been saved, and the heavy expenses borne by the Society, and the trouble and work done by the Engineers of Trinity House, in designing and erecting the apparatus have been amply justified.''

The principle had been developed by the Dutch naturalist Thijsse, Mrs Lemon added. He had been among the first to surmise that the huge mortalities, thousands of migratory birds on a single night, were caused not, as had been assumed, by collisions with the lanterns, but by the tendency of the birds to circle round and round the light until they fell exhausted. The provision of perches was an elegant solution to a bizarre but serious problem. One of the keepers involved in the earliest English experiments with the perches wrote that they became ''so crowded with birds that he could hardly

44

get a finger in between them''.

By the early thirties, land had been purchased at Dungeness; the Society's oldest reserve (then known as a sanctuary) had been established at Eastwood, Stalybridge, Cheshire, and a network of sentries, voluntary and paid, was keeping an eye on such future reserves as Sandwich Bay, Portland Bill, Ainsdale Dunes, Skokholm, Skomer, Ramsey Island and Radipole Lake, which is now under RSPB management.

In other words, the Society had clearly established a dynamic, a momentum of its own irrespective of the issue that had first inspired its foundation. But other dynamics were at work, too: inevitably, given the amateur enthusiasm that had been for so long the driving force. About 40 years on, the Society was close to collapse under the weight of its own good intentions.

It happens to all such bodies, and in many cases quite regularly, and it works like this. One maniacally motivated man or woman, or a small group of dedicated persons from whose midst a leader evolves, have a Good Idea. A 'society' is founded, and it succeeds (if it fails, that is the end of the story, or at least a different kind of story, although survival will eventually bring the membership to the same pretty pass) in realising that idea.

But by that time the organisation has developed a personality of its own, and those who are involved in its work have vested interests in carrying on that have little or nothing to do with the original ideal. This sort of thing also happens in business, of course, and in bureaucracy; I suspect, however, that the phenomenon (call it empire-building, call it ego, call it Parkinson's Law, the Peter Principle . . . it's all the same thing) is somewhat more widespread and pernicious in its effects among the voluntary agencies than in many of the other habitats that it routinely lays waste.

There is no shortage of likely reasons for the virulence of this self-destructive strain in the Societies of this world. For one thing, idealism has a dangerous habit of degenerating into ignorant self-righteousness: my strength is as the strength of ten because my heart is pure – and besides, since I am doing this job of work for the right reasons, not for mere commercial gain but in order to save the world, how dare anyone question my judgement? All too often, by the nature of Societies, the only qualification for reaching a position of great influence and responsibility therein is a belief in the cause and willingness to work for little or nothing.

Moreover, the founding fanatics grow old, and the young Turks smell their mortality. As in business, government, life, love, art and nature – but somehow it always comes as a greater shock to those who have never before had to question the purity of their motives or the quality of that which has been wrought in their name. Consequently, the in-fighting that accompanies the development of a voluntary body can be at least as vicious as anything in the nasty world of trade, if not more so. That is just one of several reasons that the very best stories about the history of the RSPB are not going to be told in this volume, nor, alas, in any other.

But there is more than enough to be getting on with. Dorothy Rook has already noted tactfully that after the first flush of infancy, ''it seems probable that the initial impetus which the Society had gained was by now dying down''. Nick Hammond, characteristically, is more blunt.

For love of birds: the story of the RSPB

"After 40 years or so," he writes, "the Society's 4,000 members could look back with some satisfaction on what had been achieved. Perhaps they even looked back with too much satisfaction. The vigorous, young people who had taken on the plumage trade and set about improving bird protection laws in the last years of Queen Victoria's reign were ageing by the 1930s. They had become vulnerable to the attacks of the young. . . ."

Max Nicholson, who himself would become one of the grand old men of the environmental movement, was among the young Turks who fired the opening rounds in the Society's first act of this eternal drama. His genius from the start was for synthesis, for sensing, defining and acting on and within a context, an attitude that we now accept as the first principle of conservation, but which then was very much at variance with the piecemeal approach that characterised, as Nicholson wrote, the Society's "exaggerated faith in sanctuaries", among other things.

Half a century later, Nicholson was to be suitably rewarded (or punished, depending on your point of view) by election to the presidency of the RSPB. Meanwhile, the book in which he launched his attack on the fustiness of conservationists in general and the Society in particular, *Birds in England: An Account of the State of our Bird-life and a Criticism of Bird Protection*, lit a fuse.

The Society was clearly unable to keep up with the times, in Nicholson's view. But worse than that, the various movers and shakers who had done reasonably if not exceptionally well over the years had become sloppy and arrogant. Branch secretaries, for example, publicly advocated views that were quite different from those of its Council, as Hammond notes:

"One of them had written to *The Times* advocating that protection be removed from peregrines because they killed other birds, and her heresy had to be publicly rebuked. Clear and strong leadership was required, claimed Nicholson. It patently was not there, when the Society was seen to equivocate on birdnesting and the shooting of birds of prey.

"By the early 1930s certain Council members began to express doubts about the conduct of the Society's administration. At its London headquarters was a staff that consisted of a secretary and two assistant secretaries, all of whom were female, helped by a very small clerical staff. The secretary, Miss Linda Gardiner, was due to retire after 35 years' service . . . In addition, a regular attender at the office was Mrs F E Lemon, wife of the Honorary Secretary, a founder member and secretary of the Watchers' Committee. Some elements on the Council felt that a man's hand was needed and that a male secretary with ornithological knowledge should be appointed.

"The idea of a male secretary was not greeted with total enthusiasm, especially by the two assistant secretaries (Miss Phyllis Barclay-Smith and Miss Beatrice Solly), both of whom felt their abilities were being ignored. Even in those days Phyllis Barclay-Smith was involved in international bird protection and was well regarded in ornithological circles. She could, therefore, perhaps fairly expect preferment. Indeed, within a few days of Miss Gardiner's retirement in 1935, both she and Miss Solly asked that they should be regarded as of equal standing with the new secretary, although they realised that he would be *primus inter pares*. If their requests were not met, they would be regretfully forced to resign. Both must have been well aware of the character of Mrs Lemon, who had recently been widowed and was Acting Hon Secretary in her late husband's place, and cannot have been surprised that such a threat was taken as a challenge. Born in 1860, Mrs Lemon was one of the founders of the Society in 1889 and, being a formidable lady, was undoubtedly the driving force in its formative years. But she could be a very difficult lady with strong prejudices and she set a high value on personal relationships, so that the action of the assistant secretaries infuriated her.

"The resignations were accepted, and the brief note Mrs Lemon wrote about them in *Bird Notes and News* did not even mention them by name. Mrs Lemon had won the first round, but the disaffection of the assistant secretaries was a manifestation of a widespread feeling in the Society that all was not well. Public airing came in February 1936 in a leader in *The Field*, then the most influential country magazine, when it criticised the organisation of the Society. This started a one-sided correspondence criticising the Council and its ability to run the Society.

"At a packed AGM in March that year awkward questions were asked by Captain Adrian Hopkins and Mr F G Bentley. The published report of the meeting went into detail about speeches by the Duchess of Portland, Sir Montagu Sharpe, Sir Henry Richards, Lords Desborough and Forester and Field-Marshal Viscount Allenby, but there was no mention of Captain Hopkins' questions about the Society gambling in real estates, inaction over cagebirds, excessive administrative expenses, the excessive ages of ladies involved with the Society, and dismissal of officers at a moment's notice. There was, however, a reference expressed as laconically as possible to Captain Hopkins' motion, seconded by Eric Parker (editor of *The Field*) that a committee be appointed to investigate the organisation of the Society. That motion had been passed, and a six-man committee set up under the chairmanship of Julian Huxley (then Secretary of the Zoological Society). Their subsequent report made various proposals for reorganisation, most of which were adopted. Some, however, were fought very hard, not least the suggestion that a fixed proportion of Council members should retire each year. That did not come about until 24 years later!

"The Society had barely settled down under the new secretaryship of Robert Preston Donaldson when World War II began. Five and a half years of hostilities did little for the day-to-day running of the RSPB whose offices, close to the Houses of Parliament, twice sustained severe air raid damage. Nevertheless, the social upheaval of wartime must have helped to spread an interest in and a sympathy for birds. Town-dwellers posted to remote radar stations, far from pubs and dancehalls, found themselves with little in which to take an interest beyond birds. The exploits of Peter Scott in the Royal Navy and the ornithological pursuits of Alanbrooke, one of the country's most popular generals, helped to make an interest in birds acceptable to many of the public. The Society's membership had fallen to 3,558 in 1942; yet by 1946 there were 6,000 members, which suggests that a large number joined or rejoined to celebrate peace."

THE PLUMAGE TRADE

(The Council of the RSPB were anxious to ascertain the full facts in regard to the present position. Last summer they arranged for an investigation to be carried out on their behalf by Mrs Rosemary Russell.

TERMS OF REFERENCE

To prepare a report on:
  (a) the past and present trade in prohibited plumage in Great Britain;
  (b) the outlook for the future;
  (c) the possibility of any infringement of the existing law;
  (d) the position in other countries.

SOURCES OF INFORMATION

  (1) the general Produce Brokers responsible for the importation of all feathers into Great Britain;
  (2) the leading firms of manufacturers and wholesalers of fancy feathers;
  (3) all the larger retail stores in London;
  (4) the leading milliners, and some of the smaller hat shops, in London;
  (5) the Investigation Department of HM Customs;
  (6) the Board of Trade;
  (7) the Port of London Authority;
  (8) National Audubon Society.

RESULTS OF INVESTIGATION
Past and Present Trade

Before 1921, the London market was the centre of world trade for feathers. Annual sales there of birds of paradise alone exceeded 100,000 and individual buyers would take as many as 5,000 or 6,000 skins at a time. In the six months prior to the 1921 Act, large stocks of plumes were built up in London. For instance, during that period one firm of brokers sold, for a foreign firm, plumage worth over £100,000; and during the period of the year following the Act, the same brokers sold for the same firm (from stocks sent over before the Act came into force and not sold outright) goods costing buyers over £150,000 – an annual total of a quarter-of-a-million pounds for one firm alone.

Apart from the business done in this way at the London auctions, there was also considerable business done direct between the trade and foreign owners.

The chief plumages of wild birds imported into Great Britain consisted of 'osprey' (known as aigrette and crosse); birds of paradise, heron, cock o' the rocks, parrots, toucans, trogons and hummingbirds; though after 1914, the trade was confined to 'osprey' and 'paradise', and a small amount of 'heron'.

Figures supplied by the Board of Trade for the Importation of Ornamental Feathers (excluding ostrich) – after 1921 these refer almost entirely to domestic and goose feathers, a fact which may be obvious when comparing the value of the much greater total weight in 1951 with say the value in 1923 – are as follows:

		Undressed	Dressed	Total
	lb	£	£	£
1919		(total lb dressed and undressed, 229,081)		272,880
1920	31,890	48,234	262,439	310,673
1921	9,748	18,093	299,630	317,723
1922	18,177	42,835	490,378	533,213
1923	35,020	6,178	449,262	455,440
1951	140,076	75,873	35,033	110,906
1952	85,149	87,472	22,316	109,788

These figures, however, paint an inaccurate picture of the true position and are wholly misleading, as prior to 1921 anyone could bring into Great Britain any quantity of plumes in person, without restriction and without paying duty. Most of the more valuable plumage was brought into the country in this way; one man, for instance, could easily carry by hand a case containing 1,000 oz of osprey (at £5 or £6 an ounce). Every week merchants arrived in this manner, and there was consequently no check and no means of estimating the quantity of stocks in the country. Those firms of produce brokers and wholesalers who might have been able to supply more accurate figures, had their records destroyed by enemy action during the war.

It will therefore be realised that when the 1921 Act finally came into force, there was a vast stock of plumage of quantity impossible to estimate held in London. But the demand for it died overnight. Manufacturers who had bought in large quantities found that there was no sale for it, and disposed of their stock at considerable loss. Much of it was sold back to the Continent: one large consignment of birds of paradise, for instance, bought at £5 each, was disposed of in this way at 7/6d each. Retail firms could have bought in any quantity, buyers report, "for a mere song": what they did buy was unsaleable and was "more or less thrown away".

Most of the English manufacturers have now closed down completely. From 1924-39 business was so bad that many became bankrupt – or closed down in time to avoid it. As each one went out of business his stocks were put on the market, so that the number of holders became progressively fewer. Most of what remained in the hands of importers was destroyed during the war years by bombing, and after the war the small stocks left were bought up by the few remaining manufacturers. This was followed by a sudden, brief revival of interest in fancy feathers after the austerity of the war years, which disposed of the stocks held by manufacturers. It is possible that there are no more than fifty birds of paradise left in the hands of the manufacturers today – probably less; and in 'osprey', a few ounces only of each of the types are held by the trade.

The exquisite nuptial plumes of several species of heron, like this great egret, almost caused their extinction.

However, demand was not only for egret feathers, confusingly called "ospreys". Hats and dresses were trimmed with feathers from all manner of birds, from the exotic plumage of birds of paradise to the humble house sparrow. The dense breast feathers of the great crested grebe were transformed into muffs; the ruff and tippets used as decorations.

There is, however, a large reservoir of plumage in private hands. Feathers do not deteriorate if carefully preserved, and a great number of women possess plumes which may have been in their families for several generations. Most of the manufacturers, the buyers in the large retail stores, and the milliners are constantly offered secondhand osprey and paradise plumes by private individuals. Few of these, however, are purchased, for public demand is practically non-existent. In many cases the owners, counting on a presumed shortage of plumages, demand a ridiculous price – usually in the nighbourhood of £20 for a bird of paradise. (With the addition of 25 per cent purchase tax, this would necessitate a resale at the prohibitive price of £30 or more.)

In consequence, therefore, of the undoubtedly large quantities of plumages in private hands, it appears probable that they will continue to appear on the market in response to any demand for some years to come.

In the meantime, most of those osprey and paradise plumes which appear on hats in public may be presumed to have been in the wearer's possession for many years and to have been 'remade' for the occasion. There are also imitations of osprey and paradise on the market, made from selected types of ostrich feathers, which are used to trim the less expensive hats; and some of these would deceive any but the expert eye.

The Outlook for the Future

It is the general opinion of all those connected with the plumage trade – brokers, wholesalers, manufacturers, retailers, and milliners – that there will never be any real revival of the fashion for wearing plumes. Among those most closely allied to the world of fashion – the milliners and retailers – there is inevitably a certain amount of conflicting opinion: some favour feather hats, others dislike them; some opine that osprey and paradise are now considered 'vulgar', others consider that every woman would buy a hat trimmed with plumes if she could afford it.

But whatever fashion may decree, there is one over-riding factor which will effectually prohibit the continued use of the more expensive plumages, or of the better imitations: the art of the plumassier is dying out. In 1921 there were 5,000 skilled workers in this trade: today there are less than 100. No girl has been trained for the trade within the last twenty years. Most of the remaining workers are aged 50-60. (In one firm one of their best hands has just retired – aged 84.)

Even today anyone already in possession of plumes of osprey or paradise who wishes to have them made up into a hat will find it an expensive and prolonged business. In another twenty years or so it will be impossible to get the work done at all: there will be nobody left in England who knows the art.

Infringement of the Law

The Investigation Department of HM Customs report that during the last ten years there have been one or two minor and isolated convictions for smuggling prohibited plumage into Great Britain from the Continent. It is very clear, however, that there is no incentive whatever to break the law on any major scale, for those who possess plumes already in this country are unable to get rid of them. There would, in any case, be nothing to be gained financially by smuggling plumes; the cost of a bird of paradise in France is about the equivalent of £20.

Nor would it be possible for any firm to handle smuggled plumes. HM Customs are entitled to examine a firm's books at any time, and evidence must be produced that stock has been in the country since before 1921. Even when buying secondhand plumes from private individuals, firms ask for a guarantee to this effect – and many of them are too nervous of the law to touch secondhand plumes from an unknown seller at all.

It is legal for a woman to come into Great Britain wearing a hat trimmed with prohibited plumage, so long as it is for her own use; but it is very unlikely that advantage would be taken of this opportunity, having regard to the limited travel allowance, the high cost of plumage abroad, and the fact that similar plumage could be obtained in England at about the same price.

Position in Other Countries

On the Continent the trade in plumage is entirely unrestricted, except in the case of France, where sales are restricted by an import quota.

Osprey at present comes from Venezuela and Brazil; from French India and Portuguese India (chiefly from egret 'farms'); and from China. Large quantities regularly reach the continental market, and there is a very brisk demand, particularly from Germany which is one of the biggest buyers.

Birds of paradise, also, sell in thousands in the course of a year, and most continental merchants still hold a stock. All plumes available, however, are old stock. There is a very strict prohibition on the export of plumes from New Guinea, and it is believed that there is no possibility of any evasion of the law in this connection.

In USA the federal tariff regulations were amended several years ago with the object of plugging certain existing loopholes, by which unlimited quantities of wild bird plumage could be imported for use in the manufacture of artificial flies for fishing, or brought in on false affidavits that they came from birds that had been 'raised in domesticity' abroad. Such plumage was then diverted to millinery uses (before the law came into force prohibiting the sale or display of wild bird plumage in New York, headquarters of the fancy feather trade, and certain other states). The only opposition to these amendments came from the fly tyers, who felt that they had been discriminated against and who said that they could not carry on business unless they were permitted to bring in additional kinds of feathers. So far they have not succeeded in getting the regulations changed, but it is anticipated that pressure may be built up when present stocks are exhausted. It is the opinion of those connected with the protection of wild birds in America, however, that no appreciable amount of prohibited plumage is being smuggled illegally into that country.

'The Plumage Trade', *Bird Notes XXVI*, 1955, No 6, pp 162-166.

The upturned bill of the avocet enables it to sweep through water and soft, silty mud searching for a variety of food items such as (a) Gammarus, (b) Palaemonetes and (c) ragworms. These creatures require special conditions particularly concerning the salinity of the water.

RSPB reserves Minsmere, Havergate and Titchwell are carefully managed to provide suitable breeding conditions for avocets. Juvenile avocet (d).

55

W H Hudson, 1841-1922

Strictly speaking the biographies of the great have little to do with this chronicle. That is to say, those accomplishments which made them great in the eyes of a more general public are reasonably well known. We know that Hudson was a pioneering naturalist, a formidable traveller, and he wrote a lot of books. The details have been raked over by legions of money-grubbing academics, doctoral students and so on. We British in any case are seldom slow off the mark in making a great fuss of our talented men and women who achieve any kind of international recognition. It makes us feel less provincial, which is far different, incidentally, from that arrant insularity with which we tend (more or less conveniently if not deliberately) to confuse it. I mean: if Hudson is the sort of thing you like, then you know all there is to know about him already – more than I can tell you, at any rate. And even if Hudson does not fall into the category of things you like, you may well know a lot about him anyway simply because he was British and well known.

So let us concentrate on the parochial, on Hudson's involvement with the Society. Mrs Lemon, as usual, is the ultimate authority.

> "My first recollections of W H Hudson date from before 1899, when he was in the habit of coming to Mrs Edward Phillips' Fur, Fin and Feather afternoons at 11 Morland Road, Croydon, at which she and her close friend, Miss C V Hall of Lancaster Lodge, London, made welcome their numerous friends interested in the protection of wild creatures; in furtherance of this, Mrs Phillips gave unstintingly of her literary ability, and great experience of the world, and Miss Hall of her money and sweet patience, the ultimate outcome being the formation of a Society designed for the protection of Wild Birds throughout the world."

Writing in 1941, the centenary of his birth, Mrs Lemon recalls that Hudson was especially partial to

> "the luncheon which preceded the afternoon's proceedings, and at which there were but two or three intimate friends; it was then that Mr Hudson talked most freely and showed us what was in his heart and on his mind; he enjoyed those

meals which were daintily served and included dishes and wines which we knew were his favourites''.

This honoured guest was nothing if not an 'inspiration', notwithstanding Mrs Lemon's caveat, ringing just a hemidemisemiquaver discordantly down the corridors of time in an appreciation published not quite 20 years after the death of its subject, that

"it was we women who had to work out the practical details and invent ways for obtaining the money necessary for such an undertaking . . .''.

Even in those days, there was no such thing as a free lunch.

Sadly, Mrs Lemon proffers no gory details of Hudson's ineptitude as Chairman of the Society. But she does note that his decision to step down and to nominate Mr, and ultimately Sir, Montagu Sharpe, JP, DL (Middlesex), as his successor "was one of the best things Mr Hudson ever did for the Society". Hudson remained a member of the Council of the Society until his death, and corresponded avidly with officers of the Society even in later life when he was seldom able to attend meetings.

A few months before his death, Hudson told Mrs Lemon that more than £6,000 was to be earmarked in his will for the Society, provided that the money was spent within two years of his death and exclusively on educational projects, which had always been close to his heart. Mrs Lemon talked him out of it on the grounds that such conditions "might lead to rash and ill considered spending". The money was left to the Society 'untramelled', although as much as possible was set aside for education.

During World War I he fretted because he was too old to fight: "feebleness he never admitted, and he set his mind, at times unsuccessfully, to elude the thought of death". When neither the thought nor the reality was any longer to be eluded, and Mrs Lemon was helping the executors to dispose of Hudson's house,

"the saddest part of this business was the destruction of all correspondence and manuscript notes in accordance with his expressed wish".

He was buried in Broadwater Cemetery with his wife Emily:

"She had been a noted singer, in Paris mostly, I believe. She had masses of beautiful hair of which he was very proud; some of his descriptions of Rima, the chief character in his book *Green Mansions*, remind me of Mrs Hudson, although I only knew her when she was old and sick."

Hudson stipulated that their memorial should be identical in material and design to that of Richard Jefferies, "the prose poet of England's fields and woodlands", nearby. The Society's epitaph, on the kerb of the memorial (a plain Latin cross in white marble on three bases): "He loved birds and green places and the wind on the heath, and saw the brightness of the skirts of God."

For love of birds: the story of the RSPB

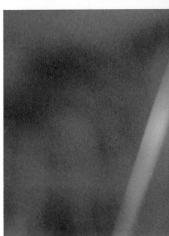

The RSPB owns or manages more than 120 reserves covering 141,000 acres. Most may be visited by the public. They are managed principally for their birdlife but frequently they provide habitat for other interesting and rare wildlife too.

Church Wood, Blean, in Kent, is famous for the nightingales that can be heard in spring, but as well as abundant birdlife the wood has a rich variety of insects, one of the main attractions being the rare heath fritillary butterfly.

Along with much of south-east England, Church Wood suffered appalling losses during the gales in October 1987, losing more than 2,000 trees. The RSPB launched a special appeal for restoration of the reserves that were damaged.

4. Land hunger

What is most interesting and important about the Society is not its origins nor achievements, its colourful leadership nor its diligent membership, nor even the specific triumphs of conservation directly attributable to its work. As a matter of fact, it is necessary to decide just what it *is* about the Society that we are celebrating, other than mere longevity, because the very decision to commission such a history is dangerous. It is much the same as deciding to write an autobiography, which always leaves the author open to the most withering of critical queries: 'So what? What's supposed to make *your* life worth reading about?'

A biography – an unauthorised biography, that is – at least suggests that someone else was already interested enough to take the trouble. But when you start writing about yourself, or hire someone to do so, you are asking for trouble. At least one of the *dramatis personae* in this chronicle, for example, has written, at quite an early age, a very long autobiography indeed; I seem to remember 800 pages, but it might only have been 400. I was unable to finish it, and so, I suspect, were many others.

In person, this gentleman is as modest and unassuming as his achievements are notable, and it has always mystified me that he could have been so conceited as to think anyone outside of his immediate family would want to know all that much about him. I suppose it was merely the arrogance of youth, and were he to reconsider the matter today, he might write many fewer pages, and figure rather less prominently himself in those pages he did manage to squeeze out past the natural diffidence that evolves with age and wisdom.

What, then, has possessed the Society to take this dangerous step? What makes it think that any but its most obsessively committed members would enjoy reading about Mrs Lemon's bad manners in the long ago; whether the offices were here or there and why, or the reasons that this achievement or that should warrant a pat on the back?

The reasons for writing the biography of a mere device have little to do with the official subject matter (except as entertainment) and much to do with the light it might shed on the grander themes underlying whatever it is the organisation thinks it is, or ought to be, doing. Those themes are numerous, in this case, not necessarily because the Society has served them particularly well, but because the implications of any conservation effort are so wide.

A wish to acquire a further understanding of what large scale conservation means in practice is one of the handful of good reasons that occur to me for buying and reading this book. Other potentially fruitful areas of enlightenment include the ways in which individual species have survived and perhaps even flourished under the auspices of the Society, among others, and the evolution of public attitudes towards environmental issues under the leadership of the Society. For a few readers, perhaps, and for no good reason, this might just happen to be the first book they have encountered about conservation. That would be nice, too, especially if the story of the RSPB inspired them to pursue the subject, and especially if these words encouraged them to conduct their affairs in an appropriate spirit of enthusiasm well tempered with cynicism.

In all fairness, the Society probably had no choice. It is a perfectly human impulse to celebrate when significant anniversaries come round, and no organisation can be immune to the human weaknesses of its constituent members. The job had to be done, the book written, whether anyone was going to read it or not.

The predicament was compounded by the fact that the best stories, as I have already suggested, are unprintable. There are even some sexy bits. The laws of the land, let alone the sensibilities of my employers and kindness to those most directly concerned, do not allow me to include any of that material, which might have made this effort the runaway best seller we all know it deserves to be. Just as well, I suppose: I have failed to make any arrangements for the movie rights.

What, then, does make this story worth telling?

NIGHTINGALES IN THE BALKANS

"The Balkan News to-day (June 22) prints an article, or portions of it, of yours on 'English Woods and Shakespeare'. And in the course of it the writer says in May-time the poet had often heard the 'nightingale's complaining note'. And so have we out here heard 'the nightingale's complaining note', but more often his joyful notes, under conditions which are worth recording. You will have a terrific tearing and roaring noise of artillery and shot in the dead of night; then there will be a temporary cessation of the duel, with great quietness, when, lo! and behold, and hear! Hearken to his song! Out come the nightingales, right about the guns, perched sometimes only a few yards from them in some bushes, in a ravine where the guns are hidden. And another kind of love music is introduced into our ears and souls, which does us good. Think? It makes you think – and beautiful thoughts come along to relieve you from the devilment of war and the men who cause it. . . ."

Letter to *The Times* (28 July, 1917) from Mr J C Faraday, reprinted *Bird Notes and News*, Autumn, 1917.

Barnacle geese on Islay. This Hebridean island is the wintering ground for up to 20,000 Greenland barnacle geese, about 75 per cent of the world's population. The geese feed on farm pastures and in recent years this has caused conflict because they have grazed on the "early bite". In 1984 the Society bought 3,000 acres (1,215 hectares) of farmland at Loch Gruinart to manage it particularly for the geese.

The RSPB was involved in a three-year-long diplomatic saga concerning another site on Islay. Duich Moss, wintering home for Greenland white-fronted geese, was rescued from the threat of peat extraction for whisky by the Distillers Group. On this occasion everyone gained and nobody lost. Tests on peat at an alternative site were urged by the Society. The tests showed that the new site satisfied whisky-making requirements: good news for the geese, the Islay whisky industry and local employment.

For love of birds: the story of the RSPB

History generates its own amusement value, of course. Especially in a country like Great Britain, a once-mighty power fallen on hard times that seem set to go on forever, whose citizens as a consequence suffer nostalgia at least as chronically as arthritis, unemployment or bad teeth. To contemplate anything that has managed to survive for 100 years is also to look back in anguish – and delight – to an era when Britannia seemed an unstoppable juggernaut and the whole world its Yorkie-bar.

The anachronism is deliberate. The Society is nothing if not anachronistic: that is part of its strength. For all the upheavals, those that can be told no less than those that cannot, provoking to this day a secret shiver of outrage among the rapidly dwindling body of survivors, the Royal Society for the Protection of Birds has managed to retain its hold on a veritable arsenal of old-fashioned virtues, however thoroughly modern the packaging. Those virtues have enabled it to flourish and prosper in a period that can only be described as conservation's Dark Ages, a period from which Britain is only just emerging as its politicians begin at last to understand that there are votes in environmental issues, and that such concerns are much too important to be left to the lunatic fringe, the ban-the-bombers . . . or, come to that, the likes of the RSPB.

If we try to imagine the Society, throughout much of its existence, as a small band of monkish types hunched over their parchments and palimpsests, their exegeses bound and unbound, only the occasional illumination striking a miraculous spark of colour now and again in the wuthering gloom, we come round eventually to the germ of a justification for this authorised biography of what is, after all, a mere bureaucratic device.

Not that they were entirely alone. There was, for example, a body known appropriately as the Farne Islands Association, which, during the early decades of the century, was among the first to recognise that acquiring land of importance to wildlife was the most effective means of controlling depredations by a public that tended to be careless and slovenly at best, wantonly destructive at worst. The association launched an appeal for funds to buy the islands, did so, and handed them over to the National Trust. Despite such resounding success, however, the principle would take many more years to become properly understood by those who stood to gain most thereby; the Society was among those responsible for keeping the idea alive and developing it until its time had come.

"The Society is also, and justly, proud of its contribution to the legislative framework in which a body of wildlife statutes has developed that is the envy of many, if not most, other nations." I quote from the work of the notional biographer of the RSPB – a character, unlike most others in this book, who is fictitious and in respect of whom any resemblance to actual persons, living or dead, is purely coincidental – who might have got the job if I had not been around, and if certain executive types (I shall spare them public embarrassment as I have spared those who featured in the dirty bits) had not had the bright idea of trying to make this book a little different. Like much of what an authorised biographer, properly constituted, must write ('warts and all', his masters would have said – they always do), that particular assertion would have been pure bombast. The policies we are discussing now evolved in large part because the law (necessary and desirable though it may be to frame laws and even more so to enforce them) was not entirely effective, and showed little sign of becoming so.

Or, as Sheail puts it rather less emotionally:

"Every effort was made to enforce the various Acts, orders and by-laws, and to educate the public in the ways of the countryside, but it soon became clear that public behaviour would not improve overnight. Public access had to be restricted on sites of high biological interest, wherever practicable, and the most effective way to achieve this was to acquire the land and control its use."

As early as 1928 the Society for the Promotion of Nature Reserves called for "far stronger deterrents . . . to restrain the unscrupulous collecting hog from uprooting all the rare plants within his reach"; and it was, appropriately, a Rothschild who, 18 years previously, had struck one of the first such conservationist bargains, in buying 300 acres of Woodwalton Fen, Huntingdonshire (home of the fen violet, among other increasingly rare species) in order to protect it. It was not until the inter-war years that the agricultural and commercial pressure on land was perceived to have become strong enough, in part because of the progressive debasement of the traditional farmer's role as steward to the land, to persuade many other than the most visionary that the virtues of ownership far outweighed the costs of buying and managing an environmentally valuable site, not to mention the notoriety that the very act of creating a sanctuary would generate.

War itself intensified such pressures, of course, and the Society, which as we have seen had taken to the principle rather earlier than many, buying up its first land in the late 1920s, was not slow to strengthen its commitment to the sanctuary or reserve principle, always with the pioneering example of the National Trust and the SPNR in its sights. (Curiously enough, a reference to The Lodge, the present home of the RSPB, surfaces in the SPNR archives, dated not long after its formation in 1912: with the death of Viscount Peel and an increase in market gardening on the grounds of The Lodge, "bonfires of heather and undergrowth were burning vigorously", a supporter complained, with dire consequences for the resident nightingales, among others.)

According to *The Times*, Sir Lionel Earle, Permanent Secretary of the Board of Works, and Chairman of the London Parks Sanctuaries Committee, has been astonished at the enthusiasm created by the proposal to set aside these sanctuaries, and by the torrent of inquiries which has descended upon him as to how such refuges can be made. The idea has indeed taken with the public in a manner that shows how little beyond a shining example and a lead is needed to stir up popular delight in wild birds as free and unmolested fellow-citizens. Especially, no doubt, does the pleasure of seeing a more abundant and more varied bird life round about its own home and haunts appeal to the non-scientific bird lover, who is too often left entirely cold by efforts to save even the most interesting of disappearing species which do not come within his own ken. The love and protection of birds not unnaturally begins at home. It has been touching to note the anxious ignorance with which information has been sought and given in newspaper correspondence, and the curious questions which have been asked of the RSPB as to the nature and results of a sanctuary. How soon would these park sanctuaries be 'put up'? What birds would come to them? Would the nightingale be heard next spring in Hyde Park? How many birds were 'turned out' to stock the place? – are some of the queries which have been put to the Society; while an eager observer remarked in one of the papers how pleasingly the presence of a blue tit in the Embankment Gardens gave proof positive of the value of the yet barely marked out bird refuges in Kensington!

WALTON HALL

The idea of sanctuaries is of course no new one. Eighty years ago Charles Waterton, who might well be adopted as one of the patron saints of bird protectors, made Walton Hall, in Yorkshire, the earliest model of its kind. The house was moated, there were ponds and swampy places in the grounds, old majestic trees, ivy-covered ruins, holly hedges to keep out cats and other poachers; and all manner of nesting boxes and holes were contrived for owls and woodpeckers, tits and starlings. Circular starling towers, on a base five feet high (a height which Waterton calculated was safe from the spring of a cat), and constructed something after the fashion of a dovecot, were built; yew hedges were specially favoured for sheltering small birds; cavities in old tree trunks were formed and shut in with doors, to attract coal tits, and an old oak was hollowed out to serve for owls. Round about the grounds was built a wall eight feet high, and this was raised to sixteen feet where it bordered the canal, in order to defy guns from barges. The very year the wall was finished came the herons, birds which Waterton especially valued, and soon established a heronry within the grounds. At one time he had his fishponds drained on account of the number of rats which infested them. On this he comments:

> "Had I known as much then as I do now of the valuable services of the heron I should not have made the change. The draining of the ponds did not seem to lessen the number of rats; but soon after the herons settled here to breed, the rats became extremely scarce, and now I rarely see one in the place. I often watch the herons on the banks of some other stone-ponds with feelings of delight; and nothing would grieve me more than to see these valuable and ornamental birds sacrificed to the whims and caprices of man."

Nowadays it is usually the greediness of the angler and the Fishery Board which seeks to exterminate this fine bird.

NATIONAL SANCTUARIES

The public and national form of bird sanctuary has come into being more recent years, impelled in many cases by the reckless destruction of wildlife by settlers in new lands. The United States has taken the lead, and now possesses a wealth of wildlife reservations, thanks to Dr Hornaday and the Audubon Societies, and also to President Roosevelt. Canada followed, owing mainly to the labours of Dr Gordon Hewitt, whose posthumous book, *The Conservation of the Wild Life of Canada*, is the finest monument to his magnificent work. Africa, Australia, New Zealand and India have also done something; but infinitely more effort is needed in all these lands to preserve not only the native birds but the whole fauna from ignorant and heedless destruction.

Great Britain has no national reserve for its surviving wildlife. The New Forest, Epping Forest, and part of Cornwall have been suggested for the purpose, but even the forests remain in a semi-protected condition. The law permits county councils to prohibit the killing of birds and taking of eggs in defined areas, but it does not empower the appointment of keepers or wardens; and without some guardianship such areas have a very limited value. In some of the more noteworthy of these (as in other important breeding grounds) the Royal Society for the Protection of Birds employs experienced watchers. For the rest, local bodies and private individuals are responsible for such bird reserves as Britain possesses.

Bird Notes and News, Vol X, 1923, No 5, pp 65-67.

World War II contributed to the development of the Society in some improbable but practical ways. Brackish marshes, for example, had been created on the Suffolk coast near Dunwich Heath, where pasture was flooded deliberately for defence reasons, and on an island at the mouth of the River Orwell, when a sluice was destroyed by a stray shell; on both sites avocets were found breeding and the Society was called in to help protect the eggs. The result was the Minsmere and Havergate reserves, where, notes Hammond, "the RSPB developed the techniques of wetland management for which it is now internationally renowned". Over the next few years, the avocet and the sites on which it had been found so caught the fancy of the public that the Society decided to ride with the tide of publicity and adopt the species as its symbol, one of many shrewd public relations decisions that have paid off handsomely in the post-war years.

Another (as any bank manager knows) was to catch 'em young: the founding in 1943 of the Junior Bird Recorders' Club boosted considerably the Society's potential for expansion, and educational activities remain among the most powerful means of recruitment. The JBRC became the Young Ornithologists' Club in 1965, and today has almost 90,000 members.

In this war year it is the duty of any adult to drag from any hedgerow or tree, by a reluctantly washed ear, every small boy he or she may see plundering birds' nests.

Remember only one boy in 100 collects a specimen egg from each nest; the other 99 smash the nests and the eggs or scatter the chicks if they are already hatched.

We are able to live in this freest of all countries, grow food for ourselves, and breathe an insect-free atmosphere *only through the activities of our rich bird life.* So I am not appealing because of the beauty of our birds or the loveliness of their songs, but because these little barbarians – the nicest of whom seem to revert to savagery at the sight of a bird's nest – are handicapping farmers *today*, apart from the more serious menace with which they are loading the future.

Roughly speaking, putting aside all love of beauty and devotion to Nature, there are two kinds of birds which are essential to our lives. One is the bird who cleans our soil and makes it possible for us to grow economic crops. This class includes such creatures as the hawks and the owls, who slaughter millions of moles, voles, shrews and field mice, and keep down the population of sparrows and other destructive birds.

Chief Sufferers

A hawk will kill and eat as many as 10,000 of these little pests in a year. Barn owls, the farmers best of friends, are believed to have been so reduced in numbers that not many years ago there were only a few thousand throughout the whole of the country.

In this same class there are the small birds who clean the soil of caterpillars, cockchafers, the deadly wireworm, which has taken an enormous percentage of the crops sown on the old grasslands compulsorily tilled since the outbreak of war, beetles and destructive insects of all sorts. These birds, which include thrushes, blackbirds, pied wagtails, peewits, starlings, and many others, are the chief sufferers from the boy vandals.

These birds are also handicapped in the good they can do, to a great extent by the modern methods of farming. For instance, in our rush to cultivate as much land as possible these days, we use three-furrow ploughs. The industrious birds can deal with only one furrow at a time, because the other two are covered up, and even then they are hard-put to catch a majority of the predatory insects because the speedy, mechanically pulled plough is upon them so quickly.

Then there are the birds who keep the air free of irritating and noxious insects and keep our ponds clean – the swallows, swifts and martins, the moorhen, the little grebe and the coot.

Again – apart from the merciless enemies, the boys – the swift, the swallow and the martin are victims of modern conditions, for in our cities, and even on our farms, iron has replaced wood so much in the construction of buildings that they find it difficult to build their nests.

The City's Vermin

The hundreds of cities and towns work against the first class of birds which I have mentioned by offering harbourage to mice and rats in tens of millions which, in open country, the birds could attack and kill.

But these things cannot be altered; the important thing is to prevent the murdering of the birds in their nests.

Never were the armies of boys stronger or more numerous, largely owing to the influx of evacuated children into the country districts. It is the duty of everyone to stop their dangerous and thoughtless vandalism.

Appeal for the Birds, RSPB Leaflet No 101, 1942.

Any chronicle of the minutiae of institutional growth is bound to have its longeurs, in narrative as in real life, notwithstanding the most valiant efforts to outmanoeuvre the dead hand of official biography. But it all adds up: the Society is, after all, one of the world's largest wildlife conservation bodies, and that counts for something. Even such unpromising material as an annual report can make unexpectedly absorbing reading, if only as an exercise in the statistics of conservation as big business.

As the public has been encouraged to get involved in the stock market in recent years, much has been written about how to read a company report. I confess myself baffled as ever; but it is much more fun when the company's 'products' are as diverse and appealing as the RSPBs. If you like that sort of thing, this is the sort of thing you'll like. It is also of its kind a model of clarity. I have chosen a year that was very good for the Society – this much, at least, I could do for my employers.

The 1984/5 Annual Report records membership approaching half a million, of which the YOC comprises just under 20 per cent. "Our strength is not merely numerical", writes the Viscount Blakenham, then Chairman of Council. "We can be very proud of the level of commitment and loyalty of our members." Loss of membership throughout the year was the lowest for some time, 9·4 per cent, and membership showed a net increase of more than 12,000. (It might never have occurred to many people, as it had never occurred to me, that large and flourishing bodies like the Society worry about this sort of thing. Of course they do.)

Staff on permanent or short-term contracts totalled about 400 with offices in Scotland, Wales and Northern Ireland; seven English regions and 103 nature reserves. Voluntary work involved 2,000 members as YOC leaders, 2,000 committee members in local groups, more than 750 Beached Bird Survey counters, 1,400 workers on reserves, and 2,000 looking after collection boxes . . . more than 10,000 in all. "This combination of staff and volunteers is the envy of our conservationist colleagues in Europe."

Political shenanigans during that year included evidence to the House of Commons Select Committee on the Environment and the Lords on Agriculture. "We also persuaded the Ministry of Agriculture, Fisheries and Foods to close a loophole in the heather and grass burning regulations."

The Society makes it clear that it disapproves of some changes in the Wildlife and Countryside (Amendment) Bill, but praises the Government's role in helping to persuade the European Community to make farming grants available "to maintain the diversity of the countryside through non-intensive practices". Significantly, perhaps, Blakenham the man, writing on behalf of a body created and nurtured by all those 'formidable women' in the long-ago, pays tribute to "our *sister* organisations in Europe" for their co-operation in the campaign to edify the bureaucrats of the EEC.

Forestry continued to be a worry, although Creag Meagaidh, a large Site of Special Scientific Interest in the Highlands, was saved by intervention of the Nature Conservancy Council from afforestation by a private company. "The tax advantages available to investors in forestry schemes make it likely that similar threats will occur." The Secretary of State for Scotland comes in for some harsh criticism, and "a stance that could best be described as 'anti-bird'" is roundly deplored. His sins are manifold, among them giving permission for peat-digging on Islay, thereby putting at risk an internationally important site for Greenland white-fronted geese. On 'flimsy' evidence of agricultural damage, licences have again been issued to shoot barnacle geese, cormorants, sawbills and herons in Scotland. In this regard the Society draws an invidious comparison between MAFF, which shows signs of learning the error of its ways, and its Scottish counterpart DAFS (the Department of Agriculture and Fisheries for Scotland). Needless to say, except perhaps in an Annual Report, the Society has made its views known to the appropriate ministries in no uncertain terms.

During that year, Lord Blakenham continues, there were exactly 7,173 birds of prey in captivity, or at least registered as such under the provisions of the Wildlife and Countryside Act, 1981. Offences against birds reported to the Society were well up from the previous year; 815 against 756. The police were involved in more than 100 of those "and the Society itself took or was closely involved in 35 prosecutions".

> "While cases concerning egg-collecting and taxidermy all increased there was a decrease in poisoning incidents, robbery of young falcons and international trade in birds. Courts seem to have imposed more severe penalties and these may have helped deter potential thieves. Another factor may have been our enlarged wardening schemes. More special protection wardens than ever were employed during the breeding season and several groups of members helped at breeding sites of rare birds."

In the spring of 1982 a pair of peregrines had settled in an eyrie at Symonds Yat, a summertime tourist attraction, for the first time in 30 years; in 1984 the Society set up facilities for organised viewing of the eyrie, and "although our publicity was low-key, 5,000 visitors were able to share the excitement of seeing these beautiful birds".

Meanwhile, the Society was unstinting in its pursuit of land on which to establish reserves, a pursuit so relentless that any commercial enterprise indulging such an appetite would have risked charges of rapacity. The Annual Report records the acquisition of four new reserves, and additions to a further nine, totalling 4,115 acres (1,665 hectares). The 103 nature reserves held by the end of the financial year covered 126,500 acres (51,193 ha) or 200 square miles (519 sq km). The most expensive purchase to date, 1,134 acres (459 ha) of Old Hall Marshes on the Blackwater estuary in Essex, cost more than £750,000, much of which was to be paid for by a memorial appeal in the name of one of the best loved Society members of all time, comedian Eric Morecambe.

A Message from Mrs Joan Morecambe

Dear RSPB Supporter

My late husband, Eric, had a very deep concern for the work of the RSPB. As a member of the Society, he played a major part in an appeal for the RSPB's splendid efforts in protecting the golden eagle.

Being so much in demand as one of Britain's best-loved comedians, he was unable to spend as much time in the countryside as we would both have liked. Recently, however, he had decided that he would like to become more involved with the RSPB – tragically, he simply ran out of time.

When, therefore, the RSPB approached me to ask whether I would agree that it should launch an appeal in Eric's name, I was especially pleased because I knew that this was a subject which would have particularly pleased him.

And what an important appeal it is.

Towards the end of 1984 the RSPB had a unique opportunity to buy what is destined to become one of Britain's foremost bird reserves – Old Hall Marshes in Essex.

This is a 1,134 acre (459 ha) area of partly-drained marshland on the Blackwater Estuary. Even now it is a terribly important place for wintering brent geese and other waterfowl – and for many breeding waders in summer. But its real value lies in the opportunities for management there which will increase the numbers of birds many, many times over.

Recently, RSPB staff showed me and our younger son, Steven, the Society's reserve at Elmley on the North Kent Marshes. I was thrilled and amazed by the spectacle of more than 2,500 birds which I saw from just one of the hides there – a sight which Eric would have simply loved to have seen, and it is this type of habitat that the RSPB wish to encourage at Old Hall Marshes.

The problem is that Old Hall Marshes cost the Society over £750,000. To realise its full potential will cost many more thousands of pounds, and all this in a year when the RSPB has had to make another crucially important, but costly purchase of goose feeding grounds on Islay in Scotland. So the Society's slender funds for reserve purchase were completely exhausted and that is why it is having to appeal for your help.

I do hope that you will feel able to help in whatever way you can.

I can assure you that every penny will be wisely spent and the result will be a sanctuary for many thousands of wild birds. At the same time I like to think that it will be a truly fitting memorial for a man who loved the British countryside.

Yours sincerely

Joan Morecambe

RSPB Eric Morecambe Memorial Appeal Brochure launched 1985.

A break-through in international conservation is also reported: the first steps in a co-operative scheme with the government of Ghana to halt the destruction of roseate terns off the West African coast. "Most of the roseate terns that now breed in Western Europe do so on RSPB reserves. We are, therefore, in an excellent position to monitor the success of any improved protection in their wintering area."

The Society, inevitably, put its oar into the long-standing campaign (since concluded successfully) to ban the use of lead weights by anglers although at that time persuasion was still the weapon of choice and results were distinctly mixed.

Lord Blakenham rounds off, understandably, with a spot of restrained gloating:

"We can look back on a year during which, despite a less than rosy national economic outlook, we managed to achieve more than ever in fulfilling the aims of our Royal Charter. That we finished in a healthy state, and with an increased membership, owes a great deal to . . ." – we can guess the rest.

All this may have happened in a relatively short time, but as we have already seen, it was hardly an overnight revolution. Among the reasons it took as long as it did was that attitudes had to change not only in society as a whole but in the Society itself. It is one thing to chip away year after year at the adamantine ignorance that we choose to call 'public opinion'; quite another thing to break with an institutional way of thinking that may have been reasonably successful for some years but is now manifestly no longer working – manifestly, that is, to everyone except those still toiling, to diminishing effect, in its shadow.

One survivor of the traumatic transition period, P H T Hartley, remembers well the change "from a 'feathered friends' society with a rather amateurish administration to a fully professional conservation body". Along the way, he recalls,

"at a time when I was trying to make people realise that the professional zoologist is not necessarily a sadistic pervert practising all manner of horrors in some locked laboratory, I had written an article for older children pointing out that to collect a series of observations and to set them out in graphical form was both valuable and enjoyable.

"I received an accusation of 'debauching the children'! I can still see my accuser shaking a trembling finger across the table."

Meanwhile, let us compare and contrast, as teachers of English used to command and probably still do, the tone of the Annual Report for 1984/5 and that of a pamphlet (as quoted by Mrs Lemon in her expurgated history) entitled *From Birds to Airplanes* and published during the War.

"The RSPB has many sanctuaries and many paid watchers in all parts of the British Isles who help to enforce the Bird Protection laws. It is interested in the studies and problems of the farmer, the landowner, the airman, the sailor, the soldier, the bird watcher, the school child, the scout, the guide, and the air cadet. It can help and advise each of them how best to identify and co-operate with the birds. Its Bird and Tree Scheme, by which thousands of school children have learned to know and love the English birds and trees, has probably done more than many Acts of Parliament to safeguard the natural riches of our native land. Five hundred and twenty different birds are classified as British and as there are over 11,000 species of birds in the world the bird watcher has a hobby which will last him a lifetime, and as he looks deeper into the life of things he will discover 'That Nature never did betray the heart that loved her. It is her privilege through all the years of this our life to lead from joy to joy.'"

It is of some significance, it seems to me, that Mrs Lemon chose this passage to kick off what was then the definitive biography of the Society, aged 54 more or less at that stage. The style is one with which we have reacquainted ourselves in this book: both convoluted and cosy, positively *fin-de-siècle* in its overtones of the pastoral and the exclusive, the lyrical and the naive; charming as ever to our jaundiced modern eye and ear, but in fact as trite and parochial as a bring-a-buy announcement in the window of a Post Office store, somewhere out there in the land of the Archers where none of us has ever set foot because it never really did exist, but which remains the spiritual home-and-heartland of the voluntary movement in Britain.

Nor is it merely coincidental, as Hammond has suggested, that Mrs Lemon's history gets considerably scantier as the years unfold. By the time she gets to the 1940s, she is

72

positively galloping through the years, finally so desperate to avoid what she would almost certainly have referred to as 'all that', that she takes a great leap back in time to the death of W H Hudson. Let us jump with her, even in this 'post-war' section of our chronicle.

"W H Hudson died on August 18th, 1922, and left to the Society practically all his fortune, as well as existing royalties on his books. On November 28th of the same year a meeting to consider the question of a permanent memorial to Hudson was convened by Mr J M Dent, and held at Aldine House; this was attended by Viscount and Viscountess Grey of Fallodon, Edmund Gosse, Muirhead Bone, John Galsworthy, Cunninghame Graham, Edward Garnett, W Rothenstein, Gerald Duckworth, H W Nevinson, and others of Hudson's friends and admirers. An Executive Committee was appointed, with Mrs Frank E Lemon as Hon Secretary. The committee's appeal for money met with a wide and generous response. In the result Jacob Epstein was commissioned to carve in marble a representation of Rima, the illusive [sic] and exquisite character in Hudson's *Green Mansions*. When completed this work was accepted for erection in a Bird Sanctuary in Hyde Park and unveiled by the Prime Minister, the Rt Hon Stanley Baldwin, on May 19th, 1925.

Independently of this memorial, members of the Society, on the initiative of Lord Lilford, subscribed money to defray the cost of a life-size portrait in oils of Hudson painted by Frank Brooks, and this striking likeness of one of the Society's best friends hangs in the board room at the Society's office; when the windows of this room were shattered in September 1940, during a serious air raid on London, this picture was fortunately uninjured."

It is clear from Mrs Lemon's peroration that there was something of an artistic flowering in the Society during these years, expressing itself in anything from the now famous Christmas and greeting cards (the first Christmas card had been published as early as 1898) to educational charts, card games and even soap. It is equally clear, at least in retrospect, that the aesthetic standards of this relentlessly ornithological line of artefacts have swung wildly from the near-sublime to the utterly ridiculous; but the object of the exercise – fund-raising – has been achieved more or less successfully most of the time.

On aesthetics, Nick Hammond, for many years responsible for the RSPB's publications, has strong views:

Art that shows wild animals is different from art that shows people (clothed or unclothed), houses, landscapes or even horses. At least it's supposed to be, but after three years' work on a book about twentieth-century wildlife artists, I am not convinced that it should be. So-called wildlife art is overshadowed by, and often confused with, wildlife illustration.

In wildlife illustration, a degree of specialisation is obviously desirable. As an editor, I learnt that an illustrator who neither knows nor understands wildlife will invariably produce inaccurate pictures. But the gulf between art and illustration is wide – far wider than many people, naturalists and artists included, realise.

73

For love of birds: the story of the RSPB

Illustrations tell you facts about an animal – that it has long toes, that it eats fish or that it is brightly coloured. They evoke intellectual responses – "I never knew that." "How amazing." "Look at the way the secondaries fall."

An illustration rarely makes the viewer uncomfortable, and her or his response to the illustration itself (as opposed to its content) is often admiration for the amount of work that has gone into the picture. This is a reasonable criterion, because a good illustrator is a craftsman, a journeyman paid to produce a finished item according to specifications.

The value to conservation of well-drawn, well-reproduced illustrations should not be underestimated: an illustrator's understanding of a particular animal can stimulate an interest that may develop and create a convert to conservation. . . .

Art that features wildlife . . . stimulates an emotional response from the viewer. The artist is sharing his experience, inviting the viewer to be as excited as he has been by what he saw. The response may be either desire – "I wish I'd been there" – or recognition – "I know just what he's getting at".

Like most environmental bodies, the Society has developed an attitude towards art that is rather more pragmatic than aesthetic: art as illustration, more often than not, for purposes of propaganda, recruitment or merchandising. As early as the turn of the century the Society used illustrations by Archibald Thorburn for its Christmas cards; but the genre took hold only with the growth in awareness of its public relations potential during the fifties, when a creative – and lucrative – relationship developed with Charles Tunnicliffe, whose works were used almost exclusively for more than 10 years. In the sixties, Robert Gillmor joined a growing stable, and as Hammond notes "the extensive use of artwork coincided with, and no doubt contributed to, the dramatic growth in the RSPB's membership from 20,000 to 400,000 in barely 20 years".

There is no shortage of theories, many of them originating in-house and most of those tending towards the self-congratulatory, to explain the development of the Society into Europe's largest conservation body. Doubtless a dedicated and efficient administration in the post-war years, plus the newly (and dearly) acquired readiness to change with the times, contributed to a growth that in the past 20 years has verged on the explosive. But public interest in and concern for conservation has also surged ahead, egged on by a series of environmental disasters on the one hand, and, on the other hand, by a succession of maverick intellectual types, by no means all connected with the RSPB, sometimes writers of books, sometimes not.

At the beginning of 1940, membership totalled 4,852, an appalling figure when taken against the 5,000-odd supporters by the end of its first year of existence, let alone the 20,000 total in 1898. By 1950, there were still a mere 6,265, and five years on only 7,000. And yet, 12 years later those numbers had increased fivefold, and more than trebled again within the next five years. By 1978 there were more than a quarter of a million, and today's virtual doubling of that figure reflects continuing steady growth, if inevitably less spectacular.

Administrative growth has been no less vigorous. The flowering of a bureaucracy is seldom a pretty sight and never an unmixed blessing, but as a growth indicator it has its uses. The structure of the Society has developed apace: regional offices, from the mid-fifties, in Scotland, Wales and Northern Ireland, while England has developed a network of its own in the North, South-east, South-west, North-west, Midlands, East Midlands and East Anglia. The hierarchical instruments of the Council with its various committees, regional committees and specialist advisory groups, complement the directorates, divisions and departments under the control of a chief executive officer responsible to the Council.

People who work for voluntary agencies tend to look askance at this sort of thing. They often choose to pursue such a career in the first place not only because there is some positive attraction (say, for the sake of argument, birds), but for negative reasons: a kind of opting out of the rat race, which is often seen in this country at any rate as largely, if not exclusively, the preserve of big business. That attitude, and the sanctimonious pig-headedness to which it so often gives suck, can and often as not does lead, as we have seen in the history of the Society, and typically of all such bodies, to collapse of stout party and disaster.

Somewhere you have to draw the line: success generates its own momentum, and it is about as sensible to complain against the changes that come with growth as to live your life in fear of death. Corporations that exist solely in order to spin money also go through phases in which the old are sloughed off like a snakeskin, only uglier, and the young are obliged to take over – are avid to take over – sublimely heedless of the fact that they will have to make all the same old mistakes before they learn all the same old lessons, and finally are cast aside in their turn.

And that is the truly dreadful thing about voluntary work: it is just like real life, and if anything sometimes worse. In fact, the saddest, most pitiable victims of business life are not the unemployed, not the unfairly dismissed, certainly not the Mrs Lemons of this world, nor even many of those whom she might have wronged, or who might have fancied they had been wronged by her, operating as they do almost to a man – sorry, almost to a woman still at that time – from a position of privilege so impregnable as to be unimaginable to most readers (certainly to the writer) of this book. No, by far the most heart-rending are those who have given it all up; who have been driven to give it all up, or who think they have – who have left responsible, well paid and respected jobs, for example, and gone to ground, as they often see it, in order to fight the good fight on the right side for a change. Those, in short, who thought they were leaving real life behind, only to find often as not that there is no escape, that their sacrifice is unappreciated and in vain. There are two reasons for this: one is that people are not always as good as they think they are; the other is that some people, at least, who are very good indeed and whose greatest pleasure in life is to get on with the job – any job – seem to become an irresistible object of dislike to their nominal superiors, whether individual or in committee. In both directions, that is what office politics is all about: 'people poisoning', as one of the more acute pop psychologists has christened the phenomenon. In voluntary organisations it flourishes, exacerbated by bad pay and excessively spartan conditions of employment, all part of the voluntary ethos. In the absence of traditional job incentives, it is often a case of those who can, will not, leaving an unstable and largely ineffectual force of incompetent idealists, most of whom detest each other, to get on with the work.

The gory details are of relatively little interest except to those most directly concerned, although it might be instructive to try to imagine the anguish of, say, a truly talented administrator who decides to give up his job at several hundred thousand a year in order to devote himself to social work licking the wounds of lepers in the East End; he then finds himself at the mercy of some moron who resents everything he stands for and makes his life at least as miserable as it was among the sharks of commerce – and without even the status or remuneration that made it all bearable.

We can only guess at how much of this sort of thing went on in the Society during its most traumatic period of transition, among the handful of staff and the progressively demoralised army of volunteers. But it must have, all of it, over and over again. The dismal membership figures, from final victory over the plumage trade until the first signs of resurgence of the mid-fifties, attest to that. But the great turnaround that followed also redounds to the credit of the Society: it had learned the hard way, but still well ahead of most others of its kind, that professionalism pays, that without it in fact, the cause, however worthy, is in mortal danger. Today the smoothly running organisation that is the RSPB undoubtedly continues to generate, like all corporations, its share of unearned personal and professional tragedy; at times, certainly, it must seem to many of its employees such a hotbed of ineptitude and rancour that it is a minor miracle anything ever gets done. But at least the remedial tools of the trade are to hand if worst comes to worst – those responsible, the company directors as it were, are always in a position to declare that they are paying an honest wage, in reasonable conditions, and are therefore entitled to expect an honest day's work.

During the fifties the Society moved slowly towards that steady state, impelled less by any miracle of self-knowledge than by the pressure of events. The Protection of Birds Act 1954 covered, Hammond declares, "almost all the points for which the Society had been struggling for most of the century". Then came the return of the osprey to breed on Speyside.

> "The attacks by egg-collectors and the impossibility of keeping the presence at Speyside of such a dramatic bird quiet meant that the Society had to announce its presence and set up a major wardening scheme."

Once again the collective genius of the Society for publicity asserted itself: "The newspapers loved the story and there must have been thousands of column inches written about the Speyside ospreys over the years." The BBC Natural History Unit was founded during this period, Hammond notes, a formidable public relations ally for anyone in the business of exploiting the public's intrinsic fascination with cuddly animals.

By 1960, the Society had regained some of its momentum. With the British Trust for Ornithology, it launched a campaign against the use of persistent agricultural chemicals that was itself to persist through the decade – another "story that received enormous coverage", helping to recruit a record 1,478 new members.

The next year the Society moved to The Lodge, a magnificent country house in Sandy, Bedfordshire, which remains its headquarters to this day. The importance of access to the Houses of Parliament and the clubs of St James's had eased as the composition of the Council had changed; London was becoming increasingly expensive and the lease on Eccleston Square could be sold at a tidy profit.

Such moves are generally calamitous for most types of voluntary organisations,

76

whose political super-egos thrive, almost by definition, on proximity to the seat of power. But although the occasional city slicker may grumble at the hour's journey to Sandy from London, on the kind of British Rail local train that evokes feelings of panic among those who dislike being out of sight of the Post Office Tower, this time the move paid off. There are two things about The Lodge that make it special: it is a lovely place to be, and there are a lot of birds about. There are also all the usual things for which corporate decisions to move house are taken: room for expansion, communications with London and the rest that are at least in theory good, and of course a cheap and suitably grateful local work force.

Hammond continues the story:

"During the secretaryship of Philip Brown, appointed in 1952, the Society had gone from a neo-Edwardian organisation to one that reflected the new Elizabethan era. When he resigned in 1963, his place was taken by Peter Conder, under whom the Society grew in influence and effectiveness as well as membership, which was more than ten times as large when he retired as when he was appointed. Supported by a far-seeing Council he set about improving the effectiveness of the Society by building up a team of staff professional in their expertise but truly amateur in their enthusiasm. Thus, by 1966, the staff included a reserves manager, an administrator, a research biologist, an education officer, an editor, a films officer, a development officer to increase membership participation and a sales officer. Membership was increasing at an annual rate of three and a half to four thousand, and stood at 31,738 at the end of 1966."

Peter Conder can in fact take much of the credit for the modern face of the Society. An outwardly modest, unassuming character with a passion for birds, he describes himself (in the tradition of the Society) as "desperately middle class' and, not so typically, perhaps, as "an academic failure" who "never passed an exam in my life".

The details of his rather remarkable life story are told elsewhere in the book; but there is one salient fact that explains many of the more notable developments during his not-quite-21 years with the Society: his family was S H Bensons, the pioneering advertising agency responsible for the world-famous Bovril campaign, and later merged with the giant Ogilvy Benson Mather. Together with Jim Alder of Newcastle, a talented speaker, artist (he later became a successful sculptor), bird man . . . and advertising man (he became the Society's first advertising agent, but his help and influence went far beyond the call of duty), Conder was in exactly the right place at the right time to concentrate the collective mind of the Society on the importance of public relations, for which it had already shown such an instinctive flair. (Can an organisation, a mere device, be said to have 'instinct'? Of course it can.)

Two other survival traits are worth mentioning: the decision taken during Conder's time, in 1960, to rotate the Council of the Society, so that infusions of new blood were guaranteed at regular intervals, and an occasionally controversial passage in the Society's constitution forbidding it from taking part in discussions of ethical issues, such as shooting and the other so-called blood sports. "That passage," Conder notes, "has saved us from the sort of dispute that has torn other groups apart."

With the appointment of a reserves manager, the Society's appetite for property

Peter Conder

He describes himself as "desperately middle-class", an "academic failure" and "a bit of a loner". He is also the Mrs Lemon, so to speak, of this century: the man who transformed the Society from a cack-handed collection of amateurs, fast running out of steam and membership, to an institution whose continued existence looks at least as secure as any of the species it has taken under its wing at one time or another.

When he joined the Society in 1954 it had 5,000 members; when he retired 20 years later, after 12 years as director, there were 200,000. He brought to the job not only a love of birds (acquired naturally enough as a nest-robbing schoolboy and sharpened during five years as a prisoner-of-war in Germany, where bird-watching was his lifeline to sanity and survival) but also – and all importantly – by the instinct for publicity bred in the bone: his family business was S H Bensons, the first British advertising agency.

For a self-confessed untutored man who prefers the company of birds to those of most others of his kind, Mr Conder speaks and writes well. (He has since acquired an honorary degree from the Open University, and his modest claims to have been less than a skilled administrator and fund-raiser during his time with the Society are similarly suspect.) Recalling his career, he starts with his first job, discounting an extraordinary seven years as warden on the isle of Skokholm off the coast of Wales, as assistant secretary.

> "The job meant I became a jack-of-all trades, dealing with reserves, prosecutions and protection work. With such a small staff, then operating from London, that was the only way. I had to travel a great deal to make surveys of reserves.
>
> We were just beginning to think of management in terms of studying the vegetation requirements for birds. I still have an old survey of Minsmere on file. This work was followed up with great expertise and ingenuity by such men as Bert Axell and moulded into the imaginative programmes we have today."

It was a time of solid progress for the Society, a time of increasing interest in television wildlife films, public concern over pollution and the state of the environment generally – and, of course, the enormous amount of publicity generated by the return of the Ospreys to Scotland.

Riding the crest of the wave was Mr Conder, who became director of the Society in 1963. One of his great triumphs in that capacity was his role in persuading the Government to take action on the use of organochlorine pesticides. The Society worked closely with the British Trust for Ornithology and the Game Research Association, who together were the first "to really collect the facts about deaths from seed-dressing.

> "Bodies of birds were analysed and a case-book presented to the Government. We kept the pressure up until the Government decided to expand departments within the Ministry of Agriculture and the Nature Conservancy, specially to study the problem.
>
> Gradually, the Government assumed more and more responsibility but there can be no doubt that the joint committee of the three organisations had a profound effect in getting these pesticides banned."

Awarded an OBE in 1976, his only regret at retirement, he said, was the failure of a project that had been dear to his heart for some time: a merger between the RSPB and the Society for the Protection of Nature Reserves as it then was. "I always felt unity would have created a really powerful and influential force in the conservation world." Perhaps. My own feeling is that the former would have had the latter for breakfast and it would have vanished without trace.

could be more effectively indulged than ever. This land-hunger, as we have seen, is open-ended, as far from satiety now as ever. Coombes Valley succumbed in 1963, Leighton Moss the following year, and Arne in 1966. The latter two were held initially on a leasehold basis; full ownership by the Society had to wait another 10 years, until the freeholds could be purchased from the proceeds of a million-pound appeal, although earlier appeals facilitated the acquisition of Vane Farm on Loch Leven, the Gwnffrwd and Ynys-hir in Wales, and land at the Ouse Washes, Cambridgeshire.

Hammond recalls:

> "The reason given in the appeal literature in 1967 for buying the Washes was its breeding black-tailed godwits. Today the emphasis would no doubt be different and the Society would appeal on the ground that it was wetland internationally important for its wintering wildfowl, because the accent is now on scarce habitats rather than individual species."

Do I detect, as a dutiful biographer myself, however I may try to resist that intolerably stuffy mantle of old bird feathers, just a trace of the dutiful about that paragraph? Is it just possible that even Mr Hammond is prey to the occasional touch of nostalgia for the good old bumbling days of the Society? After all, what would *you* rather read about: black-tailed godwits, or the Convention on Wetlands of International Importance especially as Waterfowl Habitat (1971)? When pressed on that point, he says: "Your assumption is wrong, but then so was mine when I wrote that piece. I think that we would push the godwits for their PR value just as hard today."

But the march of progress is not to be denied. Milestone after milestone passes, flicking away like the pages of a calendar in a late-night movie on television: the revamping of the children's club and the magazine in 1965 and 1966; the development of the Society's film unit (making it possibly the only such body in the country capable of producing its own films), the abolition of the old system of local secretaries and representatives, and its replacement by almost 200 local groups "involved in a variety of activities from fund-raising to beached bird surveying".

In 1970 came European Conservation Year, which was to be a monumental year for the Society, increasing its membership by more than 50 per cent at a single bound.

> "Faith in a professional approach to membership recruitment and an ability to pick the brains of experts were paying off and the Society was beginning to learn the best techniques of promoting membership."

Ian Prestt, Mr Conder's successor, was in most ways an ideal choice to consolidate and build on the achievements of previous decades as the Society expanded to become one of the nation's more formidable institutions. Mr Prestt was fortunate enough to bring to the job the formal qualifications that Mr Conder lacked: not least of all, international stature, both for his work in the Nature Conservancy and as an expert on several wildlife species, in particular the grey heron and the sparrowhawk. Consequently, the seventies and eighties have been a period not only of steady expansion, with membership more than doubling again, from 200,000 to its present half million, but also of vigorous growth in the Society's influence abroad.

5. The birds

Let us try to remember what this story is really about: not the Portlands and the Lemons of this world, nor the Peter Conders, still less, really, the Societies even. The birds are the stars of the show, and its box-office appeal rises and falls with them. It is the birds, and only the birds, that pull in the punters, enable the Society to renew and perpetuate itself as the powerful corporation it has become during the past century. Without the birds, the Society (in the view of most of its members at least, and probably its employees too) is less than nothing – an ill-assorted collection of bureaucrats messing about in the woods at public expense.

There are, to be sure, among the birds, relative constellations of stars and superstars. Their respective magnitudes, by and large, tend to increase in direct proportion to their scarcity. Not always, but often enough, the public takes a species to its heart simply because there are not many of it about. Were the human race to take a similar attitude towards its own minorities, perhaps the rest of the world would run as smoothly, and as profitably, as the Royal Society for the Protection of Birds.

The return of the osprey, for example, to Scotland during the late fifties was yet another turning point in the post-war history of the Society, and of environmental awareness in Britain. Not only was it a publicity coup that most voluntary bodies can only dream of, it also brought together so many principles of conservation theory and practice that to list them all would be in effect to create a syllabus for a degree course in applied ecology, with healthy seasonings of psychology, sociology and criminology.

Richard Fitter, in his introduction to a book on *The Return of the Osprey* by Philip Brown and George Waterston, notes that bird protection is no longer, if it ever was, a matter of "just putting a fence around an area and leaving nature to work itself out". (Despite its title, in fact, this neat little book also tells the stories of the avocet and the black-tailed godwit, with passing reference to bittern, marsh harrier and others, some of which never did come back and show little promise of doing so.)

Fitter continues,

> "It is clear that bird protection falls into three main categories: protection against human law-breakers, protection against natural predators, and preservation of the habitat."

The latter was even in 1962, when Fitter wrote, and remains today, by far the most difficult and expensive. Marshland is the worst of all. "Drainage of marshes is the first step towards bringing land into cultivation, and most marshes are surrounded by sluices and dykes that take away the water you are trying to keep in. Where the sea is involved, too, as with the avocets, which must have brackish lagoons to feed in, it is even more difficult, because all the engineers' efforts are normally devoted to keeping the sea out, not to letting little bits of it in."

Left to its own devices, the osprey breeds in Europe, ranging from Scandinavia to the Mediterranean and in fact has a world-wide distribution. By the end of the last century, a combination of egg-collecting and shooting – what Philip Brown, a fairly excitable character by some accounts, describes as a persecution "often characterised by an almost satanic malevolence" – had reduced the British population to two, possibly four, pairs, which soon disappeared. "It was assumed," writes Ian Dawson, senior librarian of the Society, in an unpublished history to 1982, "that the osprey had become a permanent loss to our breeding avifauna".

From the early fifties, however, sightings of the species in Speyside suggested at least several abortive attempts to breed. It is now thought likely that birds were present and breeding each year from 1954 and possibly from 1952 until the first confirmation of an eyrie in Sluggan Pass in June 1955. In 1957, the Society, which had been involved, inevitably, in a frustrating attempt to find, confirm and decide what to do about any breeding pairs that might have turned up, mounted 'Operation Osprey'. Dawson continues:

> "In 1958 a pair of ospreys refurbished an eyrie at Loch Garten and laid eggs. Plans were put into operation for a 24-hour guard, and all seemed to be going well until two-thirds of the way through the incubation period when an intruder climbed the tree at night, presumably with the intention of stealing the eggs. However, he was spotted, and only just managed to make good his escape, in the process dropping the two osprey eggs, having substituted hens' eggs in the eyrie. After a few days' unrest by the birds this deception was discovered. The ospreys then moved to another tree on the other side of Loch Garten where they built the by now familiar 'frustration eyrie'. Thus all the carefully laid plans had been thwarted, although valuable experience had been gained that would prove useful in future years."

Those of us to whom a bird is a bird is a bird may have some difficulty appreciating the 'frustration' of the human beings involved, let alone the ospreys. The operation had in fact been conducted like something out of a spy story by Somerset Maugham, complete with coded telegrams (the code word for imminent breeding was 'Inflation'), and secret encampments, as much to prevent inadvertent disturbance of the nesting pair (lest crows nip in and steal the eggs while the parents wheeled overhead shrieking at some blundering birdwatcher) as any more sinister activities. But even after all that secrecy, before the very eyes of Philip Brown and Bert Axell, one of the collectors got in, did his worst, and got away. "We reckoned we had missed catching the intruder by 50 yards or less", Brown wrote in *The Return of the Osprey*; ". . . another 15 or 20 seconds".

The next year, the Society took no chances. Both the original nest tree and the repeat, 'frustration' tree were doctored: the lower branches were sawn off so that the trunks could not be climbed easily, and barbed wire was bunched around the bases of the trunks. The small army of wardens – tents, field telephones, *et al* – took up their positions at the first tree, and the birds duly returned, almost to the second.

82

But this time all was well. Dawson reports:
"Three chicks hatched in early June and shortly afterwards the RSPB, at George Waterston's insistence, made the major decision of publicising the event through the media. It would only have been a matter of time before the news leaked out, and this decision to actively publicise the return of the osprey was one of the RSPB's masterstrokes."

Philip Brown generously remarks that he was "quite horrified" by Waterston's proposals, and "I must record that I advised against such a course . . ." But "it was a decision which has been fully justified by the results".

Not that the ospreys were entirely, as it were, out of the woods. The chicks had barely hatched when a forest fire broke out at Nethybridge, within a mile of the eyrie. Wardens joined the firefighters until a shift in the wind drove the flames away from the nest.

During the remaining month and a half of that breeding season, the Society and its precious charges became the toast of the media. About 14,000 people came to see the ospreys that year, and more than a million since, as 'Operation Osprey' has been repeated annually. In 1969 Loch Garten became the centre of a reserve that now totals 2,949 acres, and there are now about 30 breeding pairs of ospreys in Scotland, raising about 50 young each year.

Birds of prey are in a sense the exception to the rule that even the most nondescript species becomes interesting if it is scarce enough. The raptors, as Waterston writes, "with their masterly powers of flight and their swashbuckling mode of life are the most exciting and romantic of all our breeding species". They have exerted a fascination throughout recorded history: from the middle of the twelfth century until the seventeenth especially, they were strictly protected in the interests of falconry. "It may have been due to this protection that they were then so common throughout the country and probably reached their peak in numbers in the sixteenth century." But then came the perfection of the shotgun, the large-scale husbandry of game birds, and, of course, the Victorian passion for collecting, skins no less than eggs, which led to decades of slaughter affecting virtually all species.

The osprey in particular was known to Aristotle, and Waterston quotes a rather off-putting passage in Leviticus:

"And these are they which ye shall have in abomination among the fowls; they shall not be eaten, they are an abomination: the eagle and the ossifrage, and the ospray."

Shakespeare wrote in *Coriolanus*: "I think he'll be to Rome, as is the Osprey to the fish, who takes it by sovereignty of nature"; and in a play by George Peele it is proclaimed

I will provide thee of a princely osprey
That, as he flieth over fish pools,
The fish shall turn their glistering bellies up,
And thou shalt take thy liberal choice of all.

Ever since the osprey returned to Scotland in the late 1950s after an absence of over 40 years, thousands of people each year have travelled to Scotland to see this magnificent bird. The RSPB's public viewing scheme at its Loch Garten reserve has attracted well over one million visitors.

Since the 1950s, the Scottish osprey population has steadily increased to more than 30 pairs. The recovery has not been easy, the birds at Loch Garten have attracted more than their fair share of disasters, from egg-collectors to vandals in 1986, when the topmost branches of the nesting tree were sawn off. Rescue work meant a rapid reconstruction of the tree (above), and the female osprey soon accepted her rebuilt nest, although breeding was unsuccessful that year.

For love of birds: the story of the RSPB

James IV of Scotland is said to have trained an osprey to catch fish, and the species was kept, with cormorants and otters, in special buildings on the Thames at Westminster at least as late as 1618. The very name 'osprey', incidentally, distantly echoes of the infamous plumage trade, and is according to Waterston, a corruption of the French 'esprit', describing the feathers.

Curiously, Waterston writes: "I can find no published records of an osprey swimming." He has compiled his accounts, he observes, from something like 3,400 pages of notes taken by more than 100 people in three years of constant vigil at Loch Garten.

The Osprey Camp 1959: the late Group Capt Dawkins, Frank Hamilton (RSPB Director, Scotland) and the late Eddie Balfour.

The Dutch have a word for avocet: *kluut*, which describes its call in time-honoured onomatopoeic fashion. Kluut – which to me has a solid, reassuring sound to it, quite unlike the rather twee 'avocet' – turned up fortuitously during the late forties at two wetland sites in Suffolk which were to become among the most important of the Society's reserves.

I have never had a lot of sympathy for wetland birds. It seems to me that their favoured habitats are on the whole rather disagreeable places, neither land nor sea, highlighting the more inhospitable aspects of the various elements which conspire in this case to make them a bit of everything and nothing much of anything. In temperate climes, some wetlands might have their moments, when the light is just right, insects are at a minimum, and the human observer, if such there must be, has found himself a reasonably dry tussock or hummock or whatever, something at any rate that doesn't squelch when stepped on. But as for the tropics, or a British wetland in summer, surely there can be no more unhappy a place for man or beast on the face of the earth.

86

It all goes back to the salubrious qualities of relative sterility: the principle that less nature is more. There is no escaping man's (western man's, at least) instinctive abhorrence, for all the lyricism he devotes to recalling it, of high summer, when the exuberance of the life force reaches life-threatening intensity. All Britons should be forced to read the American poet Wallace Stevens's evocation of Hell: heatbound stasis, overripe fruit on the verge of putrescence, change and decay, and all that sort of thing . . . or, for that matter, to reread, in the light of what we *really* feel about nature, Galsworthy's description of the death of a Forsyte: "Summer, summer summer! The soundless footsteps on the grass!" Both of these towering *aperçus* at least appear to have been perpetrated on dry land, *terra firma*; wetlands in that context would have been beyond description.

That which makes wetlands so attractive to birds, of course, is just what makes them so uncomfortable and repellent to us: the fact that they squirm with living matter, positively boil with it. Like most animals, birds have extremely unappealing personal habits. Just consider the way bits of slugs, insects, garbage, chewed-up rats, rotten vegetation, are regurgitated – vomited, in plain English – into the voracious mouths of the chicks. There is rather more of all that in a wetland: or come to that (let us mince rats if we must, but not words), a mire, morass, slough, swamp, bog, or as a matter of fact, an ancient word but delicious, slobland. Some of these rough synonyms have acquired precise ecological definitions over the centuries, but basically they are all much of a muchness: slurry by any other name.

Considerations of why the avocet chose to absent itself from such places in this country, however logical the decision might seem to me, must remain speculative. "Too much emphasis has probably been laid upon the drainage of the fens", writes Philip Brown. He notes that the eggs were not bad to eat, and therefore "many a potential avocet probably ended up in an omelette". Others were eaten whole, or were stuffed, and so on until, by the mid-nineteenth century, they had disappeared as a breeding species, although for several decades they continued to be seen (and shot) as visitors or migrants.

It was always fairly certain, however, that the protection afforded the species by the Dutch, just across the North Sea, would eventually result in their re-establishment in the British Isles. (A one-off nesting by two pairs in 1938 in County Wexford, Eire, hundreds of miles from their normal breeding range, took everyone by surprise.)

As it happened, the birds turned up at two separate locations in Suffolk, Minsmere and Havergate, in 1947. Two separate groups, the Society at Havergate and a small band of ornithologists at Minsmere led by Lt-Col J K Stanford and his brother the brigadier (plus a captain and a major, if you please), protected the two colonies quite independently and for a time totally without knowledge of the other. Col Stanford later wrote of this

"most striking instance of what bird-protection can, and should, be, not a matter of Acts of Parliament and schedules hung on police-station walls, but a combined effort by people living in their own countryside to save, it may be for one year only, or it may well be for posterity, some portion of the beauty in our marshlands which our forefathers too often allowed to perish".

The story of the peregrine is well known and illustrates the value of birds of prey as "indicator species". Its decline in the 1950s and early 1960s alarmed conservationists and contributed to the discovery of the hazards presented by the pesticides such as DDT used in agriculture.

Today, the peregrine's population has recovered to almost pre-war level, but the birds still face pressure from egg collectors and illegal falconers. In 1983 more than 70 peregrine nests were robbed.

The young bird on the left is "evidence" in a prosecution, about to be returned to its home territory.

Secrecy tends to surround many peregrine eyries, but one, at Symonds Yat, a popular beauty spot in Gloucestershire, has been well publicised. In 1984, the Society arranged an observation point to show the public nearby breeding peregrines. It was a venture so successful that it has since been repeated with other bird species, including great spotted woodpeckers and kestrels.

For love of birds: the story of the RSPB

It was at least partly in connection with the avocet that the Society pioneered some of the techniques of reserve management, which one writer, in yet another unpublished history, has described as "large-scale gardening". Management is especially necessary in wetlands, which tend to be 'transitional' habitats: that is to say, terrain which is in the process of changing to something else. Many a wetland, left to itself, would quickly become overgrown, as vegetation took hold, creating scrubland, then woodland, until that which attracted so many of whatever species it is we are worried about had vanished, to become just another patch of countryside.

In the best of all natural worlds, this would not matter a lot: most landscapes are always shifting around and changing, so that as one habitat vanishes another develops somewhere in the vicinity. But reserves are by definition 'islands' in an alien surround; such isolated sites cannot possibly survive if nature is allowed to take its course because there is no place for them to go, no truly natural environment beyond the boundaries which have themselves been created artificially. Reserves are, because of this island status in a sea of hostility, peculiarly vulnerable in much the same way that real islands are – to introduced predators, for example, or untoward influences generally from the great beyond. Therefore, they must be managed, not only because management makes them better reserves, more attractive to more species and more capable of supporting those species, but because if they are not managed, they will perish.

There is nothing at all new about this, as a quick browse through any history of husbandry or landscape development will confirm. The most reliable techniques have been inherited from the past. Woodlands were being 'coppiced' from the year dot; grazing animals like cattle and sheep are used to this day, as they have always been, to control habitats (many of them on reserves managed by the Society) that might otherwise revert to an earlier state; and ecologists (not to mention the curious folk who used to live in such places) have known for many years that there are better and worse ways of treating habitats that contain a great deal of water.

That having been said, modern engineering techniques, combined with large helpings of quite sophisticated chemistry, physics and geology, have been conscripted into the never-ending battle, a battle, ultimately, against nature, albeit on nature's behalf. It does not help that those same disciplines have yielded, initially during the last war with its urgent need for increased food production, methods of reclaiming land that at one time would have been considered 'marginal' – that is, fit only for those relatively small human populations capable of working it one way or another, usually in the context of an ages-old tradition, but otherwise strictly 'for the birds'.

One result, as John Crudass, chief reserves officer until his retirement in 1984, has noted, is "that the value of a reedbed or other type of habitat is no longer what it is but what it might become. No more than in any other walk of life will a landowner dispose of a capital asset at a figure less than its maximum, and conservation bodies have had to accept this hard fact of life and rid themselves of the foolish idea that choice sites could be preserved on the cheap".

The would-be reserve manager is in a curious position. He, or his organisation, must justify a large capital outlay in order to deploy techniques that are seldom very different from, and are often identical to, those at the disposal of the previous landowners or would-be developers, in order to repel the forces of nature on the one hand and encourage them on the other. At the same time, potentially productive land, as the non-conservationist world measures such things, will have to be kept if not actually rendered unproductive, and its guardians may even have to try to influence events beyond its borders if such events threaten any adverse effects on the little bit of heaven that is being so assiduously cultivated within.

So, clearly, the decision to buy or lease a reserve is not taken lightly. Although quite a few of the Society's reserves were set up for the benefit of one rare or endangered species, that is not the best reason, and in any case it transpires more often than not that a habitat which is good for one species is good for many. During the early seventies, the Society worked out a set of criteria for assessing the relative importance of reserves: the value to the natural world in general and to mankind (and bird-people) in particular of different habitats, species and ranges. One of the principles was to achieve a good mix among the various reserves, so that one way or another the Society might be able to account, like Noah, for a self-perpetuating paradigm of everything that mattered.

The Society defines 20 ornithological habitat types in the British Isles, each with its distinctive bird community. Bird species are defined as 'typical' (occurring more or less continually throughout a clear range of habitat) or 'local'. Breeding species can be common, rare or occasional; bird populations can also be categorised in terms of whether they breed, overwinter or merely pass through, and whether their numbers comprise given percentages of regional or world populations. Reserves are bought if possible, leased if not, but only provided the leasehold is at least 21 years and includes management rights. It is not always necessary for the birds to be present at the start: the potential of the habitat, under proper management, may be enough. It helps if the Nature Conservancy Council has already listed the property as a Site of Special Scientific Interest (SSSI), or can confirm that such listing would be appropriate.

The habitat definitions are quite fun, and taken together could almost add up to one of those pastoral poems so beloved of the types who assisted at the birth of the Society. Consider:

> Rocky isles and stacks; rocky coasts, cliffs and cliff-tops!
> Sand dunes, shingle, low offshore islands. . . .
> Mud. Sand flats. Saltmarsh.
> Brackish water; mud?
> Coastal grazing marsh, lowland river systems.
> Flood meadows.
> Reed swamps. Lowland lakes and reservoirs.
> Gravel pits.
> Upland river system; northern marshes,
> Upland pools and lochs.
> Dry moorland. Bog.
> High montane, heaths – mixed upland broadleaf.
> Mixed lowland broadleaf.
> Native pine forest?
> Open canopy broadleaf!

The birds

A warden's life does not involve constant birdwatching. RSPB wardens have to be versatile and resourceful. Here are a few scenes from recent years:

(a) A cement truck falls through a plank bridge at Minsmere (1980);
(b) Clearing rhododendrons at Coombes Valley (1978);
(c) Repairing a stone wall: Les Street on Islay (1984);
(d) Building a boardwalk at the Dinas (1972);
(e) Attending the Warden's Conference (c. 1974). From left to right: Cliff Carson, Mike Blackburn, Steve Madge, John Partridge, John Hunt, Maurice Waterhouse, Graham Williams, Richard Wakely, Norman Sills, Ray Hawley, Anthony Chapman, Bob Scott, John Day, John Wilson, John Crudass, Russell Leavett, Andrew Grieve, Peter Makepeace, Peter Gotham, Bobby Tulloch, David Mower, Michael Walter, Doug Ireland, Martin Robinson, Alan Parker, Rob Berry, Peter Conder, Tony Pickup, Bryan Pickess, Jeremy Sorensen, Peter Bowyer, Dick Squires, Terry James, Mike Everett, John Humphrey, Roy Dennis, Jimmy Dunbar, Nick Dymond.

For love of birds: the story of the RSPB

On second thought, perhaps just a bit *avant garde* for Mrs Lemon's taste, but still not so far off the mark. Edifying, a shade lyrical, and a more or less accurate reflection of reality as perceived in certain quarters. All this helps to prepare us to read, for example, Minsmere's technical specifications.

Minsmere is where much of this large-scale gardening technology first saw the light of day. It is an SSSI and a reserve of international importance, comprising 1,500 acres of reedbed, muddy lagoons, woodland and heath with a rich variety of breeding, passage and wintering birds.

The reserve is famous among those who take an interest in such matters for 'the scrape': not a new dance craze, but a deceptively simple means of extending both the extent and the lifespan of a wetland habitat. A scrape is basically a shallow excavation in the drier areas of the marsh into which the flow of water is controlled so that there is enough plant and animal life to support the birds through as long a breeding season as possible. The engineering problems can be formidable: controlling salinity, for example, as the artificial bodies of water swing wildly between evaporation and flood. Afficionados of the scrape argue, nevertheless, that it often creates conditions which are even better-than-natural, a line of reasoning that must surely apply to any successful reserve management technique, within the constrictions (and they can be quite severe) of the island ecology that limits and defines the reserve itself.

A scrape can be as small as one acre; Minsmere's is over 45 acres, and breeding pairs of various species in that part of the reserve have increased from 40 to more than 1,500 since the idea of a scrape first took hold in 1959.

The flooding of the Minsmere Level during the war had left an ideal marshland; but about 50 acres were too high to retain water and had grown unpleasantly and unproductively rank over the years in the absence of grazing. The proximity of the sea opened an opportunity to create a slightly brackish lagoon, a worthy addition to a reserve that already contained a good mixture of habitats in wet reed-marsh, heaths, woods and dunes. Terns as well as avocets were expected to respond with enthusiasm.

In 1962, a bulldozer made the first two-acre pilot excavation in the middle of a stand of couch-grass, leaving three islands of clay surrounded by brackish water. The smallest of the clay islands was covered with gravel taken from an Ice Age deposit elsewhere on the reserve in order to attract terns. A pair of common terns duly arrived and nested, the first at Minsmere since 1950. The Society carried on scraping, year by year, for the next decade, until it had what it wanted.

Minsmere, Suffolk
TM473672   *1,500 acres*
SSSI, NCR1*. Reedbed, muddy lagoons, woodland and heath with rich variety of breeding, passage and wintering birds. Mainly in the parish of Westleton, 4 miles north of Leiston and 6 miles north-east of Saxmundham.
Management Invasion of the open heath by trees is controlled by selective thinning-out of Scots pine and birch. The woodland's natural regeneration is retarded by rabbits and therefore long-term maintenance must include planting

young trees. Oak, beech and hawthorn are planted and sycamore, bracken and rhododendron are removed to improve the structure by opening the canopy to allow improved growth of the herb and shrub layers. The small area of pasture is maintained by licensed grazing and haymaking for the benefit of the flora and breeding snipe.

The reedswamp that is such a feature of the reserve has to be controlled. The reed must be prevented from invading the open meres and ditches, and trees must be prevented from invading the reedbeds. This is the most intensive, regular management carried out on the reserve.

One habitat, the Scrape, is man-made. It is a combination of shallow water, wet mud and small islands of varied surfaces – shingle, moss or grasses. It was created using heavy plant and a large amount of back-breaking human effort. To retain the open wet mud, so important for waders, management must be intensive, because it is a fertile area for plants. Care must also be taken over the control of water levels and their salinities, so that optimum conditions for wader feeding can be maintained. Vegetation on the islands has to be managed to remain suitable for breeding terns, avocets and other waders.

Birds Over 300 species have been recorded and about 100 breed each year. Between the middle of May and the end of July is an excellent time for an evening walk along the public footpaths on the heath to enjoy the churring nightjars, roding woodcock, owls and smaller birds such as the tree pipit and stonechat. It is in spring, before the leaves become too dense, that there are the best views of nuthatch, the three woodpeckers, nightingale, redstart and most of the other songbirds to be expected in southern England. Where the woodland meets the wetland edge, Cetti's warblers can be heard singing.

The 400 acres of reedbeds are wonderful for birds throughout the year. Bittern, marsh harrier, bearded tit and water rail are regularly seen. From the tree and island mere hides there are good views of warblers and wildfowl. Occasionally a spoonbill or a purple heron might be seen on the edge of the reeds and kingfishers as they fish from suitable perches near the hides.

The Scrape is ideal for gaining close views of breeding terns, avocets and other waders. Since it was made, forty-six species of wader have been recorded here. From April to mid-September there is good birdwatching here, but it is in late summer and early autumn when there is a mixture of plumages – summer, winter, adult, juvenile or a combination of any of these – that the fun of identification can really be enjoyed to its fullest.

Plants The large heathland is largely ling and bell heather with patches of gorse and bracken. A natural succession of Scots pine and birch with some oak and hawthorn is spreading into the heath. The woodland originates from 19th century game coverts and is mixed with oak and Scots pine dominant and sweet chestnut, sycamore, hazel, birch and beech are very noticeable.

There is a small area of pasture with a marvellous array of plants such as ragged robin, bog cotton, yellow rattle, marsh stitchwort, lousewort, various clovers, marsh orchids, interesting grasses, sedges, and rushes. In the surrounding ditches grow water violet and pondweeds. While common reed dominates the reedbeds there are odd patches of bulrush with a sprinkling of willow, oak and hawthorn and a large

For love of birds: the story of the RSPB

A major threat to birds in the UK is that posed by the blanket afforestation of the Flow Country in the north of Scotland. The wild and lonely moors are the home of nationally important populations of greenshank, golden plover, dunlin and merlin as well as other scarce birds such as red-throated divers (right) and golden eagles.

The foresters could not lose in one cause célèbre concerning the Creag Meagaidh Site of Special Scientific Interest in the central Highlands. The site was purchased by Fountain Forestry who attempted to obtain Forestry Commission approval to plant, and caused a furore amongst conservationists (Creag Meagaidh was seen as an important test case). Ian Prestt in Birds magazine (Winter 1983) said,

*"It would seem . . . that some firms at least intend to challenge
the Nature Conservancy Council's view that to preserve the
high nature conservation importance of this site it must
remain unplanted". The NCC in fact stepped in to buy the
site, but Fountain Forestry made a profit of £130,000 on the
transaction without even planting a tree.*

97

amount of marsh sowthistle.

Invertebrates   The variety of habitats provides a good number of insect species. So far identified are over 300 species of moth, twenty-four butterflies and sixty-six species of beetle.

Mammals   Coypu are often seen on the meres and another, more unwelcome, escapee from fur farms has been recorded here, the American mink. Otters are present in winter and sometimes breed. Also in the marshes are the abundant water voles, prey of the marsh harrier. Harvest mice nest in the reeds and feed in autumn on the nuts of alders. Three species of shrew are present. Red deer are rarely seen because they hide in the woods during the day, but they come to the reedbed to feed at night. Brown hares can be seen feeding on the new saltmarsh vegetation on the Scrape.

RSPB Nature Reserves, RSPB, 1983. Sponsored by Mobil North Sea Ltd.

Another kind of management, at the Dungeness reserve in Kent, has paid off financially as well as ornithologically. There the excavation of gravel has created jobs for the locals, revenue for the Society . . . and, of course, an enhanced habitat for the birds, many species of which find gravel pits much to their liking. The Society hasn't gone quite so far – it would not dare – as some reserve managers in the Netherlands, where species that are both plentiful and edible, such as wild duck, are 'harvested' and sold to help cover costs; but a tidy little profit on the side from management work that would have to be done anyway is practical conservation as high art, and a fine example of a principle I shall define in the next chapter: 'convergence'.

To be fair, that sort of management is probably far more easily achieved in some habitats than in others. Woodlands are among the more easily turned to some kind of profit: The *Birds and Broadleaves Handbook*, a rather technical book on woodland management published by the Society in 1985, notes that our earliest exploitation of the forests was bound inextricably with an understanding of its value; so that "even while man was actively destroying the wildwood he was still dependent on it, particularly for fuel and building materials". It is quite likely that, in areas of southern Britain that were relatively densely settled even before the Roman colonisation, there were woodlands which had been spared from clearance specifically to provide a sustained supply of needed materials. Some of our forestry skills have a British pedigree several thousand years long.

> "Certainly by the time of the Norman Conquest, woodland management skills were at a high level. By then, most of the wildwood had disappeared and what remained was largely in active management."

Much of what remains is to this day in active management, by the Society among others, and revenues from a well-managed woodland can go a long way towards defraying the costs of maintaining it. The Prince of Wales, who among other things is the President of the Royal Forestry Society of England, Wales and Northern Ireland, told its Centenary Conference on Forestry and Conservation in 1982:

> "Good forest management, it seems to me, means working with nature and using

it as part of the management process rather than against it."

Not that the Society is always so lucky. Occasionally, even the most seemingly logical management technique can backfire in totally unexpected ways. One delicious little scandal developed several years ago when the British press discovered that the Royal Society for the Protection of Birds, no less, was culling populations of a few of the more common seabirds on some of its reserves in order to give less favoured species a chance to breed. The case of the "poisoned seagulls" ran for weeks and caused a small flurry of membership resignations – even though the use of that technique had been common knowledge for some years, at least among those who bothered to read the literature freely distributed by the Society. But it was a good story.

The return of the black-tailed godwit to the Ouse Washes during the early fifties was also a good story, albeit less obviously exciting than, say, the Osprey Saga to those who can take godwits or leave them alone. Like the avocet, they just turned up and the Society came tearing round to see what ought to be done about it. In this case the main threats to the new arrivals were not men (the field in which they settled was both privately owned by a sympathetic farmer and fairly remote), but cows, which tended to trample the eggs, and carrion crows, which given half a chance would eat them. Still, publicity could have proven troublesome.

Peter Conder sums it up:

"There are a number of ways to protect a rare bird breeding in this country. One can either leave it severely alone and hope that nobody else finds it. This has the disadvantage that if anything goes wrong, one does not know the reason. It would be satisfying to know if the bird has successfully reared young. But this is really only a secondary consideration. The alternative is to set up a rigorous guard. This of course takes time and money and does attract undesirable publicity. If it is done properly and discreetly there is little chance that the birds will be disturbed. Or one can follow a middle course: to guard the nest and ward off the dangers but at the same time keep sufficiently well in the background to avoid attracting publicity."

Leaving the bird severely alone, Conder continues, is suitable only for those species that breed in Britain most irregularly; such as hoopoe and green sandpiper. But "once a bird becomes a regular breeder, although only in small numbers and in restricted localities, the dangers of discovery increase enormously". The critical point is the spread of the species to enough different sites that extermination becomes unlikely, however widespread the publicity. A relatively recent example is the collared dove, "which has swept across Europe and whose spread it would be virtually impossible to stop".

The black-tailed godwit took quite a while to reach that state, however. Conder, writing ten years after its first known nesting, still felt obliged to conceal the identity of the RSPB member who first discovered it; and although its status is far more secure today, the decreasing numbers of wetland habitats in Britain make it likely that the Society's initial strategy will always apply to some extent: "to keep an eye on the

99

breeding success but in such a way as not to excite public interest''. If you want my opinion, this objective is rather less difficult with the black-tailed godwit than with a lot of other species I can think of.

For a start, the reintroduction of the sea eagle to Scotland is shaping up to be one of the more dramatic conservation successes of the century. Vicious persecution by farmers, for reasons that owed more to ancestral superstition than to the dictates of natural history or agriculture, combined with the progressive poisoning by insecticides first discovered during the fifties, to reduce even its European breeding population to alarmingly low levels. Only Norway, with about 350 pairs at that time, by far the lion's share, had enough to be worth mentioning.

Until 1983, the last reputed nesting of the sea eagle in Scotland was on the Isle of Skye in 1916, and the last British bird, an unusual white specimen said to be 30 years old, was shot in Shetland two years later. The attempt to reintroduce the species has a more honourable history: as early as 1968, the Society brought four young birds from Norway, reared them on Fair Isle and released them. All the birds died or disappeared, but the effort was renewed, largely under the auspices of the Nature Conservancy Council from 1975 on the island of Rhum, and about 100 birds have been released to date, with a survival rate of about 50 per cent and the first successful nestings in the wild from 1985.

BITTERN

Where the joy of watching

It seemed like a good idea at the time: to spend a week as a voluntary warden at one of the 80 bird sanctuaries run by the Royal Society for the Protection of Birds. Voluntary wardens can be of virtually any age, assuming reasonable health; in return for their labour, they are granted spartan accommodation and a cheap, healthy, working holiday in the nearest thing to a wilderness the United Kingdom has to offer. I chose the Leighton Moss Reserve at Silverdale, Lancashire.

Leighton Moss, with 400 acres, is one of the Society's smaller reserves, although it virtually adjoins one of the largest, 6,000 acres, at Morecambe Bay. It is a habitat of reed beds and willow scrub in a valley surrounded by limestone hills. Every reserve has its 'star turn' and Leighton Moss has the bittern. This is the only area in northern Britain where it still breeds. Otters also frequent the reserve. I knew none of this when I arrived but learnt fast. I kept a diary.

Saturday

Four hours from Euston, I start as I mean to continue by turning the wrong way outside the station; 20 minutes later I have reached the reserve, which is 100 yards away. I am shown to my 'chalet', more like a Portacabin, in a thicket of reeds and willows. I am lucky in my accommodation: alone, when I might have had to share with as many as three; a fridge, a fan-heater and – most unusually – a shower in a toilet block in the main reserve building.

As I expected, the warden is somewhat taken aback to learn that I don't know one end of a bird from another. He suggests I spend the afternoon familiarising myself with the reserve and report for work at 7.15 tomorrow morning. I visit the hides: hushed, clapboard chapels in which the faithful congregate (today is one of three or four visiting days a week) in their ceremonial anoraks peering at the objects of their devotion through narrow slitted windows. In the brilliant afternoon light I have this irresistible feeling that what I am really doing is watching Regent's Park on television.

My cooking, which will get progressively more disgusting as the week progresses, is on a Calor gas range: dehydrated soup and a sausage, with bread, cheese and an apple. Afterwards I fancy a drink. The nearest pub is a mile down the road; it's a long way there, and a longer way back. . . .

Sunday

Raw and misty. Up at 6 am for 7.15; the chief warden and I are going to take a bird census in a wood. This, I learn, is done largely by ear; the cacophony of songs and calls gradually resolving into separate strains. I founder through marshy woodland, past coppiced willows and huge waist-high tumuli of tussock sedge, struggling desperately to keep up with the warden.

He is a stocky, cheerful man nearing 50 and seemingly of inexhaustible energy; he never walks when he can bound, never bounds when he can run. He doesn't like it when I call the visitors 'punters'; we are expecting a lot of them today, because the spring tide in Morecambe Bay will drive the waders high on the shore and well into binocular range. Having visited the shore, the punters will then make a day of it by descending on us in their coachloads.

The only serious problem this influx is likely to cause arises from their tendency to crowd into one particular hide, which is apt to tilt dangerously over the water when full. One of the voluntary wardens then has to stand outside and turn them away.

In the afternoon I sort through some rubble for path-building (more of this later), sand down some windows for painting, and clean up a workshop. I see a greenshank. It's asleep.

Monday

I fell asleep to the booming of bitterns, a very rare sound in Britain, and much like the sound a far off giant might make blowing across the top of a milk bottle. Nobody warned me that birdwatching is best done very early or very late in the day: this day will stretch from 7.15 am to 9.32 pm.

This morning's census-taking is in the reeds, and so I make the acquaintance of the 'Burma Road', a diabolically tricky path cut through the middle of, well, a swamp. The warden, who carries on bounding, is delighted with his take; sedge warblers, reed warblers, whinchat, wheatear, buntings and plenty of bearded tits, one of the star turns (together with bitterns, otter and deer) of this reserve.

They all look alike to me; small and fast moving, dots on my bleary horizon. Stumbling back we carry willow logs on each shoulder; left over from the coppicing, they are beginning to sprout and would be safer and more useful in the woodpile. I have to admire their dogged, doomed perseverance. My own patience is fast running out.

The warden's wife runs me into town for some shopping, which includes a much needed walking stick. This is the object of some amusement. "You'll lose it in the mud", she says dourly, more than once.

More censuses in the afternoon – butterflies this time – and more walking; followed by several hours of shovelling limestone rubble into wheelbarrows for the paths. These paths, connecting the various hides, tend to be washed away each winter and have to be built up again in the spring. This work is done routinely and incessantly, whenever there is a slack moment between other chores.

In the evening I visit the lower hide, a round trip of three miles. I am transfixed by the glorious evening light, all golds and blues, through the slitted windows. I see a bird, and consult my bird book. After 20 minutes or so of anxious riffling I realise that what I am looking at is a heron.

The sunset turns mauve, and in the far distance I see a vast amoeboid flock – starlings in their thousands – pinpointing the exact moment of dusk as they roost. This is explained to me, as is the presence of sand martins – another series of fast moving dots. Odd how they dart about just like the gnats (or is it midges?) on which they feed.

Tuesday

My feet hurt. I never realised how much sheer plodding is involved in 'managing' a reserve. This one – more than 300 acres plus another 4-6,000 acres on Morecambe Bay, is quartered by the warden and his assistants every week; surrounding areas, where possible, are also censused regularly. All that takes place in between the heavy work – coppicing, reed clearing, those confounded paths – much of which is done perforce during the winter. Whatever the time of year, the work is never finished; enthusiasm in such circumstances is a survival trait.

A trip to Morecambe Bay by car (unaccustomed luxury) yields two surprises: a pair of mute swans nesting in a building site, and a flock of plover settling on the shingle and seeming immediately to vanish, so perfect is their camouflage. The swans, carrying on swanning amidst continuing uproar, squalor and mounds of industrial spoil, have become a *cause célèbre*, with locals demanding an end to all activity until the cygnets have fledged. In fact, the birds' apparent aloofness and indifference to their surroundings seem to sum up the ultimate futility of the conservationists' cause. With my own survival in mind, I keep as mute as the swans.

For dinner I surpass myself with the most appalling concoction of leftover cauliflower, day-old haslet, rice and mushy peas. I put most of it out on the makeshift bird table behind the chalet; it is (wisely) ignored.

Wednesday

For the first time I wake up not wishing I were dead. Feeling positively fit, in fact. Outward Bound for grown-ups, I decide.

I help shepherd a party of schoolchildren from Stockport around the place. I have trouble telling the teachers from the kids. The birds are becoming less of a problem: fewer than a dozen species seem to visit the hides regularly at any given time of year, and most of them are large and easily distinguishable as waterfowl or gulls. I'm still hopeless at songbirds, however.

In the late evening I see an otter, thus becoming one of the very few in this country ever to have done so in the wild. Even the author of one of the authoritative otter books is said to have seen only one, once. It looks a bit like a seal at first, undulating through the water in the middle distance under the last pink vestiges of a windy sunset; more a presence than a sighting. Later still, I go visiting, and meet the man who wrote the music for the Martini commercial. He's a local academic; they are fairly thin on the ground in this neck of the woods, too.

Thursday

I see a bittern, also an unusual sighting. Like so many of the elusive famous, in the flesh it is a bit short on personality. A brownish sort of heron, which just stands there, a smudge in the reeds.

An ordinary heron, a much more elegant and charismatic character, catches and eats a duckling. It takes an uncomfortably long time to die, and even longer to swallow. Old dears, I am told, tend to get a little upset at such manifestations of nature red in beak and claw. On such occasions cries of "Can't you do something?" and "shoot it!" have been known to reverberate through the hides.

A group of red deer frisk, unusually, in the open: two hinds and two yearlings, with the summer red coat just beginning to show through.

Friday

I come to grief on the 'Burma Road' and sink into the mud above both wellies. This seems to please everybody but I am not amused. Why anyone would subject themselves to all this for a silly little bird like the bearded tit, which won't even sit still, is beyond me.

In the afternoon four of us travel by tractor to the limestone quarry and load a five-ton skip. Then we go back to the reserve and unload the entire skip into wheelbarrow and onto the paths. Ten tons: I still can't believe it.

Saturday

Cleaning up the chalet and packing for the train to Euston, I notice a female chaffinch on the bird table outside. This strikes me as a happy ending, on two counts: above all because it must mean that the male, which has been scolding, chattering and generally pestering me all week, has at last found a mate; and secondly because ... well, I identified it, didn't I!

The Times, 2 October 1982, by Tony Samstag.

Chaffinch from Bird-catching and Bird-caging – RSPB Leaflet No 57.

6. Convergence: Politics, professionalism and the law

One of the hardest lessons of the century has been that conservation is good business. It may cost money to begin with, but the return is most often swifter than expected and almost never negligible. To discuss conservation in terms of business sense is to return to environmental first principles: the appeal to self interest.

It was Max Nicholson, among others, who first disseminated the definition of 'convergence' as this curious phenomenon in which opposing interests so often end up talking about the same things and finding themselves on the same side. Past a point in any discussion of environmental conflict, the various issues begin to come together and with them the apparently conflicting aims of those engaged in the dispute. The most obvious and compelling examples are in industry, where the arch-polluter is brought round to the idea that by cleaning up he will not only get any number of pests (such as the Society) off his back but will also make more money: he will run a cleaner, more efficient operation, and most probably will be able to sell the waste products he has cleaned up. Just as one man's weed is another man's flower, one man's poison, properly collected and refined, is another man's stock in trade.

An instinctive understanding of convergence – in business, politics, law – is very often the secret ingredient in one conservation body's success as against the dithering away of others to oblivion. Some agencies, foremost among them perhaps the World Wildlife Fund, have exploited the principle to its hilt, building on carefully nurtured Establishment ties to raise money, most notoriously through flamboyant sponsorship schemes, with much the same fervour as the RSPB acquires land. That particular route to organisational prosperity seems to have been relatively unexplored by the Society, but with notable exceptions. For example, the indispensable but distinctly uncommercial *Birds and Broadleaves Handbook*, which tells you everything you ever wanted to know about some of the more technical aspects of woodland management, was published in 1985 with the help of a grant from BP – like so many oil corporations, desperate to project a corporate image as a closet Friend of the Earth. Similarly, the Eagle Star Insurance Group was persuaded to underwrite a series of RSPB initiatives on behalf of eagles (including a book, a film and the protection programme for the reintroduction of the sea eagle), which it has in turn exploited through its own publicity campaigns. Another instance, as we have seen, is profit from reserve management work that would have to be carried out in any case.

The commercial aspects of convergence might well be something to pursue more aggressively during the next hundred years. Where the Society has excelled up to now, however, is in politics and law. Like all voluntary agencies in this country, the Society labours under the conceit that its work must not work in a political way. That is the charity law, and it is rigidly enforced. Transgressors can lose the favoured tax status that makes it possible for most such bodies, 'registered charities', to function at all. But common sense no less than history is clearly on the side of the campaigner, and not all great Neptune's ocean can clean from any organisational hand the legalistic stain left behind when it behaves, as it must from time to time, as a pressure group.

That the Society and others of its ilk can get away with such monkey business at all is some evidence of the strength of the conservationist cause – and of 'convergence' – which makes it possible for the population in general and the Charity Commissioners in particular to take a benevolently narrow view of what 'politics' really means; in fact, to have brought about an evolution in the relevant statutes whereby some political activities are defined as more or less political than others. The political activities that are permissible must be 'ancillary to a charitable purpose' or they may be undertaken in response to an invitation by the Government to comment on legislative proposals. A Member of Parliament can approach a charity for information, and in certain cases the charity can lobby an MP for support of its cause in Parliament. There are other very fine lines to tread – or unravel as the case may be – and one rather splendid loophole: private bills are considered "free from taint of political activities". There are, of course, partisan considerations in the definition of activities as 'political' or not; in this respect, perhaps it is just as well that Britain has never developed a Green Party of any size or influence, so that mainstream conservation campaigning at least has managed to steer clear of legal complications which have shackled many no less idealistic organisations concerned with, say, Third World development or domestic social issues.

The law, as we have seen, can be also both the object of a campaign and a device for the use of the campaigners. Turner observes that

> "for much of the present century, the laws which were supposed to protect birds, especially wild birds, were a loose mesh of anomalies, pierced by scores of well worn loopholes".

The Society – which, remember, had from the beginning identified proximity to Westminster as a priority for the choice of its headquarters – had fought until 1921/22 to get through Parliament the Act banning the importation of plumage, and trap pigeon-shooting persisted until that same year. Even in an apparent era of dawning enlightenment, moreover, a Departmental Committee on bird protection could still contemplate the caging of wild birds and conclude:

> "Properly safeguarded, we see no reason why the practice should be accompanied by cruelty and many wild birds do in fact live in captivity in perfect health for long periods."

Warming to its theme, the Committee went on to praise the keeping of caged birds as providing many town dwellers "with an innocent solace and amusement". There was "no reason for its general abolition". It was not until 1954 (the year of the Duchess of Portland's death as it happened, after 65 years as President of the Society), that the Protection of Birds Act finally outlawed the practice of trapping wild birds, along with

105

For love of birds: the story of the RSPB

so many other practices against which the Society had campaigned (in its capacity as a registered charity, of course) for so many years.

As so often in this chronicle, the redoubtable Mrs Lemon is a handy authority for official developments. The majesty of the law arguably first weighed in on the side of the Society with its incorporation by Royal Charter in 1904, after barely 15 years of existence. But as early as 1902, Mrs Lemon notes with approval, "some useful legislation" had been added to the Wild Birds Protection Act of 1880, and

> "a Customs circular promulgated in British India 'to prohibit the taking by sea or land out of British India of skins and feathers of all birds except (a) feathers of Ostriches, and (b) skins and feathers exported *bona fide* as specimens illustrative of Natural History'".

The Society had already, in fact, been instrumental in bringing about an Army in Council Order of 1899 abolishing heron plumes from the headgear of officers of the Royal Horse Artillery, Hussars, Kings Royal Rifles, and Rifle Brigade.

Mrs Lemon notes, with understatement which may or may not be deliberate (she must have had a sense of humour, but it is not often on show), that

> "notwithstanding the Bird Protection Acts and Orders in force at the close of the last century, it was evident that some of the rarer British birds were becoming alarmingly scarce. Amongst those chronicled in 1901 as having vanished as breeding species were the ruff and reeve, marsh harrier and honey buzzard, whilst some eighteen other species were feared to be in danger. . . .
>
> "This was a matter of grave concern to ornithologists and bird lovers, and active endeavours were immediately made to check this woeful depredation of British avifauna. One useful step was the passing of the Wild Birds Protection Act of 1904 which provides for the forfeiture of specimens illegally taken."

By this time the Society had already appointed its first 'watchers'; Foula and Hascosay in the Shetlands were among the first to be patrolled, and by 1914 there was a network of 10 districts, with 22 men employed under a Watchers' Committee. A series of local county council orders, meanwhile, was building up precedents for protection of birds and their eggs that would eventually be incorporated in national law.

Hammond writes that

> "site of the first battle for legislation was in Yorkshire – at Bempton Cliffs, now an RSPB reserve. Here in the 1830s the elements of commercial exploitation, cruelty and ignorance met on board a steamer that took parties of up to 30 'gentlemen' beneath the cliffs. As the steamer hooted the seabirds took to the air in fright and faced a barrage of shot".

Charles Waterton, a Yorkshire squire, naturalist and author, lived nearby. He

> "was not averse to shooting interesting specimens for his collection, but was appalled by the senseless destruction of the birds and moved by the fate of the young left to starve on their ledges, which he described in his *Essays on Natural History* (1838)".

Convergence: politics, professionalism and the law

The British Association for the Advancement of Science took up the case, after a persuasive address by Professor Newton; a powerful group of clerics came together in order to combat accusations that the slaughter was perpetrated by local people (the group was called the East Riding Association for the Protection of Seabirds and was led by the Vicar of Bridlington, the Rev H F Barnes-Lawrence); the RSPCA brought its formidable influence to bear, and so to Parliament.

Black-necked swans – dead on arrival at Heathrow   one of the photographs that supported the RSPB's report into bird importation, All Heaven in a Rage, 1974.

The first piece of wildlife legislation for the protection of wild birds, then, was the Sea Birds Preservation Act of 1869. It was also one of the few Acts of Parliament ever to grant protection for its own sake, that is to say on account of a principle not directly related to person or property. But it was virtually unenforceable and far too limited in scope, even in the context of public outrage at the plumage trade and the *battues*.

The Wild Birds Protection Act, which followed in 1880, at least set a precedent in extending a notional protection to most other species, although it was no more potent than its predecessor. And, as Philippa Bassett notes in a private study in 1980, both Acts "drew the attention of the public not only to the destruction of birds for their plumage, but also to the increasing incidence of other forms of cruelty to bird life and to overcollecting of birds and their eggs". (Egg collecting was grandly known as 'Oology' at that time, and natural history societies thought nothing of organising 'oological expeditions' or advising members on the appropriate display cabinets, pipettes, egg-drills and the like.)

With the involvement of the Society, the pace of legislation quickened: the Wild Birds Protection Act of 1896 gave county councils the power to apply for orders to protect particular species and habitats; subsequent Acts in the first decade of the century allowed illegally taken birds or eggs to be confiscated, banned the use of the pole trap and the teagle, and established close seasons for scores of species. In 1925 the Protection of Birds Act banned the use of bird lime and the practice of using birds as decoys. Philippa Bassett continues,

"Many of these and other unsuccessful bills were drafted and introduced or directly instigated by the RSPB, which had considerable support amongst MPs. Yet despite this wide range of legislation, the RSPB still considered it inadequate because there was no element of compulsion for councils to provide for the protection of birds, and because it considered the 'White List' principle as introduced by the 1880 Act to be a very negative way of approaching bird protection."

For love of birds: the story of the RSPB

The 'Black' versus 'White' argument persisted until 1954, when the comprehensive Protection of Birds Act swept the distinctions aside along with most of the previous legislation, and extended automatic protection to all birds unless otherwise specified. Today only species listed on Schedule II, the 'blacklist', may be killed, by authorised persons.

It is more than the law that has changed, of course: it is the whole of society, its attitudes, priorities and preoccupations. Hammond ruminates to splendid effect on the theme:

> "A hundred years ago bird protectionists were a small ill-organised bunch of guerillas who struggled against the massed ranks of privilege, vested interest, greed and blatant disregard for wildlife. An interest in natural history was for years a sign of eccentricity. That the will of Lady Glanville, a notable seventeenth-century entomologist whose name is commemorated in the Glanville fritillary, was contested on the grounds that her interest in butterflies was evidence of lunacy is today surprising."

Even Squire Waterton was thought a bit strange because of his interest in birds: despite the intervening Age of Reason, Hammond continues – but "perhaps also because he insisted on wearing his school uniform even as an adult".

The process of convergence is never-ending, as a glance at any issue of *Birds*, the Society's magazine, will show – and the Society is still in the thick of the legislative process, exerting a far from subtle influence on the deliberations of the Mother of Parliaments whenever such activities are deemed necessary. One successful recent campaign concluded with the banning of lead in anglers' weights (because of the huge numbers of swans suffering from lead poisoning as they gobble up the metal along with the grit essential to digestion). Vigorous campaigns continue over forestry policies and their allegedly destructive effects on traditional habitats. There is also the unfortunate fact of life, already touched on more than once in this narrative, that a law on the books is not necessarily the last word; so that the Society often finds itself campaigning for the effective enforcement of various statutes long after it has won the battle to create those statutes in the first place. How many policemen have the ornithological expertise to enforce even the Protection of Birds Act 1954 (one of the most complex Private Member's Bills ever put through Parliament), let alone the all-embracing Wildlife and Countryside Act.

The most comprehensive piece of legislation the Society has ever had to face was, in fact, the Wildlife and Countryside Act, 1981. Its passage set a number of records and near-records in Parliament, too. The Bill contained no fewer than 70 clauses and 16 schedules, occupying more than 110 pages, and it took 11 months to work its way through the legislative system, by which time it had attracted more than 2,300 amendments. The Society was only one among almost 100 organisations consulted by the Government during this marathon, and the preliminary consultative process alone, during which the Department of the Environment circulated a series of 'information papers', took a good two years.

That uniquely British ambivalence towards charities comes into relief in such circumstances. Although their charitable status prevents the Society and its ilk from campaigning to change the law, such bodies are permitted – expected, indeed – to respond to Government requests for advice and consultation, and to make their views available to MPs and to their own membership once a Bill is published. And individual members of a charity are of course free, as ordinary citizens, to react as vigorously as they wish to any proposed Act of Parliament within the limits of entirely different sets of laws, such as those defining public order.

Stuart Housden, head of the Society's conservation planning department, recalls: "From the information papers it was clear that the Government's initial approach, particularly on the protection of wildlife habitat, was inadequate or even, in the case of some of their plans, downright alarming. . . . The most important and contentious subject in the Bill that the RSPB had to tackle was the future of wildlife habitats – after all, there is little point in protecting wild birds if you allow the very places upon which they depend to be destroyed."

The issues were, inevitably, something of a mind-boggler to the non-conservationist public, meaning almost everybody, or so it was thought at first. But the man and woman in the street, not to mention their elected and hereditary representatives, soon proved themselves remarkably adept at struggling with such concepts as Sites of Special Scientific Interest, of which there were about 3,800 at that time, and some of which the Government proposed, in rather Orwellian fashion, to designate 'more special than others'. The Society was one of many to argue, persuasively in the event, that such discrimination would ultimately mean the destruction of the less favoured sites.

Mr Housden continues: "On 16th December, 1980, the Bill received its second reading in the House of Lords, which proved to be a most interesting and far-ranging debate. Over the Christmas period the amendments to the Bill began to pour in – so that by the time the Bill entered its Committee Stage in late January several hundred had been tabled. The level of interest surprised and alarmed the officers of the House. . . .' Significantly, too, the national press for once appreciated the magnitude of public interest in this piece of legislation, so that even the most blinkered news editors were obliged to reflect the importance of the Wildlife and Countryside story in their pages.

The debate also created news in a very real sense. The core issue of the Bill – whether habitat protection was to be governed by voluntary guidelines as the Government wished, or by statutory controls over farming and forestry operations – provoked a flood of information, alarming, even sensationally alarming, statistical information of the sort that is almost impossible to disprove, so that it is equally beloved of news editors, their audience and environmentalists, too. The nation drew breath with a kind of prurience at the intelligence that 30 to 50 per cent of ancient and semi-natural woodland in Britain had been destroyed since 1947; that almost a third of designated SSSIs in the county of Dorset alone had suffered damage during the one year 1980 . . . in short, that the end, yet again, was nigh, indeed even nigher, than the Cassandras of the lunatic fringe had been insisting for so many a long and weary year.

The end product, which required yet a second Act to tie up the loose ends, was inevitably a compromise, but not a bad one. The Wildlife and Countryside Acts, as we now know them, are a veritable paradigm of environmental legislation in that they are capable, at least in theory, of dealing with virtually any domestic conservation issue that is likely to arise. They are as close as we British are likely to come to a constitution for conservation – and birds in particular are exceedingly well looked after.

But not even this most awesome monument to the legislators' art has been able to improve that invidious situation in which the Society is so often forced to act as policeman, taking the law into its own hands, through private prosecutions and through vigilante-style activities worthy of a television thriller which few individuals or non-governmental organisations could hope to get away with. Once it starts, there is indeed no end to 'convergence'.

The process is if anything likely to accelerate in the immediate future, as British politicians of all parties come to a belated understanding that the passions of their constituents on environmental issues run strong and deep. Although the evolution of a Green Party on European lines is most unlikely in Britain (and, given the theoretical constraints under which conservation 'charities' operate, might actually be undesirable), there is no turning back the environmental education of our policy makers. It has taken them a long time, and Britain has a long way to go before it no longer deserves its description (with the exception of its exemplary bird protection legislation) as 'the dirty old man of Europe'. But the way ahead could well be easier than at any time since our instinct to exploit nature first began to recede, in the face of an impulse to protect it.

It will be interesting to see how the Society evolves. It has already changed from an anti-cruelty movement to an organisation concerned with species protection, and then again to a giant landlord preoccupied with habitat conservation. Perhaps in time a truly cosmic attitude will prevail, and the birds themselves will be relegated to the deliberations of some sub-committee or other in the Royal Society for the Protection of Absolutely Everything Worth Protecting and the Abolition of Everything Else. This may not be exactly in accordance with the letter of the Royal Charter, but it is certainly a trend in the conservation movement – and our politicians know it, and it scares them half to death.

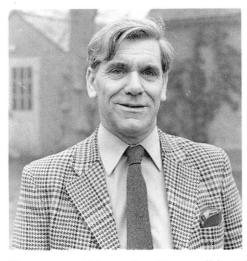

John Crudass

His name will be unfamiliar to all but the most obsessively knowledgeable in British conservation; but John Crudass, who retired in 1984 after 16 years with the Society, probably wrought more (and longer-lasting) changes in the natural environment than most of those better known personalities who have coruscated through these pages.

Reflecting, perhaps, the growth of the Society as an institution after those early years in the perfervid grip of a clutch of agitated women, his career details are scanty and low-key: 'A Bureaucrat's Progress', albeit with a very happy ending. Mr Crudass was Chief Reserves Officer. It was his responsibility, as Sir Derek Barber, Chairman of the Countryside Commission and himself a vice president and former Chairman of Council in the Society, wrote in announcing the retirement,

> "to seek out properties as potential RSPB reserves, argue his case through RSPB Council, negotiate purchase or leases with owners, appoint wardens and manage, in highly sophisticated ways that he pioneered, the woods, islands, marshes and moorlands that rapidly accumulated under the Crudass regime".

Having encountered a warden or two in my time, I can guess at the strength of character manifest in Sir Derek's description of

> "his deft and sensitive touch with his wardens . . . a delight to behold; it was a mixture of the avuncular, the military – he was once a very young adjutant – with a strong touch of the guide, philosopher and friend. Those allowed in to his Warden's Conferences, a remarkable honour accorded to very few, found the experience akin to being received as a guest at the most exclusive of clubs."

When Mr Crudass joined the Society, it was the owner of six reserves; at his retirement, it owned or managed more than 100. Enough said, except by the Queen, who subsequently awarded him the MBE for his pains.

7. Pollution and pesticides

There are a few, exceedingly few, baleful influences on the environment that turn out, with time and experience, to be less destructive than at first was thought. Oil pollution has been one of those very rare instances: the recuperative capacity of marine habitats has in this decade astonished scientists, conservationists and all who thought that what the French so evocatively describe as 'the black tide' spelled everlasting doom for life, the universe and everything.

The dawning awareness that such was not inevitably the case generated a feeling of cosmic relief, as if mankind, after all, were not quite so pernicious as he had been made out to be, and oil (which is, after all, itself a product of the earth) not quite the unmitigated man-made nemesis it had appeared as *Amoco Cadiz* followed *Torrey Canyon* into racial memory.

Nothing is quite so simple, of course, nor so reassuring; and many birdlovers however perspicacious and dispassionate, are not always so disposed toward the long view. For them the constant threat of a major pollution incident, not to mention the constant recurrence of minor ones, is a nightmare from which there is no awakening. In 1979, in a foreword to its definitive report, *Marine Oil Pollution and Birds*, the Society noted that

> "the most obvious and certainly the most emotive outcome of marine oil pollution is its effect on seafowl.
>
> "Indeed, not infrequently, the only visual evidence that an oil slick has passed by offshore is the appearance of oiled birds on our beaches – sometimes dead and so heavily encased in oil as to be scarcely recognisable for what they are, sometimes still alive, struggling ashore unable to fly or dive but making valiant, futile attempts to preen their contaminated plumage."

The first recorded oil pollution incident in British waters involved the *Thomas W Lawson*, which sank off the Isles of Scilly in 1907, killing seabirds and fouling the shores of Annet with oil from her tanks. The story of attempts to prevent similar incidents was a chronicle, the Society declared in its report, of "over 70 years of failure". By the end of 1918, Mrs Lemon adds, "bitter complaints reached the Society of the toll taken of birds, the world over, by floating oil, great patches of it, sometimes miles square, in which sea birds became entangled and rendered helpless".

Shipwrecks, of course, were regrettable enough, particularly as the loss of life they occasioned was seldom restricted to birds. But it soon became clear

112

"that not only were wrecks responsible for this pollution, but that all oil driven ships when at sea discharged refuse oil whenever their tanks were cleaned out".

The Society was quick as ever to rise to the occasion:

"After ascertaining that ships could be fitted with separators which would obviate the necessity of any oil being thrown overboard, and the names of firms which had perfected and supplied such apparatus, appeals were addressed to every navy in the world, and to all known shipping companies, and ship owners, imploring them to fit their ships with separators, the adoption of which had been proved to effect substantial economy, as the oil extracted could be returned to the tanks for further use."

It was an early example of convergence, in other words, and of a professionally international approach, with appeals sailing all over the world in French, German, Italian, Spanish and even Japanese translations. The Bibby Line achieved immortality of a sort, in Mrs Lemon's Pantheon at least, by being the first to oblige, and to fit separators to all its ships. But as the campaign gathered momentum, so the international ramifications of the problem became more apparent. Not even the passage of the Oil in Navigable Waters Act of 1922, making it an offence to discharge oil in UK territorial waters, could be counted the major triumph it should have been, because it extended no farther than the three-mile limit. The Society lobbied, successfully, for an international conference on oil pollution; but the delegates converged on Washington in 1926, talked their heads off, folded their briefs and stole away virtually empty handed. By 1934, the UK had managed to raise the issue in the League of Nations, but with similar non-results.

Although most countries now subscribe in theory to a network of treaties and protocols, primarily under the aegis of the United Nations, in practice deliberate releases of oil continue, and efforts to control it or even to cultivate a less lackadaisical attitude towards accidental spillage, are commonly almost as ineffective as in Mrs Lemon's day. For example, the International Convention for the Prevention of Pollution from Ships, in 1973, rashly sought, "certainly by the end of the decade", the "complete elimination of marine pollution by oil . . . and the minimisation of accidental spills". It seems most unlikely, in retrospect at least, that the nations concerned had any intention of reforming their slovenly habits in time to meet that deadline, so the deadline was revised instead. Perhaps next century sometime, surely . . . ?

The Beached Bird Survey, which was organised by the Society from 1966 to 1985 as an *ad hoc* monitoring operation involving many hundreds of people, mostly volunteers, also proved invaluable for the collection of data on species distribution and population trends, irrespective of its original purpose. Internationally, perhaps the most enduring achievement to date attributable to the fight against oil pollution has been the establishment of the International Council for Bird Preservation, an estimable body and not nearly as well known as it might be. Sadly, what with the inevitable muddles between RSPB, ICBP, Preservation, Protection . . . a fine example of bureaucratic word-blindness at its most impenetrable.

Pollution and pesticides

Seabirds are among Great Britain's richest wildlife assets. Twenty per cent of the world's population of gannets nest in the British Isles – they can be seen on the RSPB reserves of Bempton Cliffs in Yorkshire, Humberside and Grassholm, Dyfed.

Oil pollution is one of the major hazards to seabirds. Gannets were victims of oil spilt from the Christos Bitas *off the coast of Wales in 1978. More usually, surface-swimming birds such as the guillemot (below) are affected.*

For love of birds: the story of the RSPB

The Society draws four 'key lessons' from the dispiriting saga of its global campaign to control oil pollution:

"First, it is extremely difficult to make progress through international law in its widest sense. If the UK is to protect itself from oil pollution, it must look to its own resources and those of neighbouring states. One key issue is the failure to extend UK control over an area of territorial sea more relevant to modern threats than the range of an 18th century cannon-shot.

"Second, the great majority of shipping and oil companies have been most reluctant to accept preventive controls which involve financial penalty. The principle of 'polluter pays' does not apply when any equity and much of the cost of oil pollution continues to be borne by birds, marine life, the holiday industry and coastal local authorities.

"Third, many ship-masters continue to ignore national and international laws and codes of practice which regulate oil pollution at sea. Economic factors encourage them to do so. Fourth, without effective enforcement, even the best laws will be valueless."

The Society has tended to keep away from such operations, arguing that the survival rate of oiled birds, however apparently successful their treatment, is low, and preferring to work towards a policy of prevention rather than fire-brigade action once the preventable accident has occurred.

As any alcoholic knows, one poison leads to another. By 1928, the RSPB was warning in *Bird Notes and News* against the overuse of arsenical sprays in gardens, orchards and fields. During the early sixties, the use of persistent organochlorine pesticides was recognised as one of the main factors in the decline of birds of prey populations – Rachel Carson's *Silent Spring* (1962) alerted much of the world to the danger – and they were banned in many countries.

The campaign to ban such pesticides in Britain was inextricably linked to the decline, fall, and resurgence of another of those winged superstars that have served the Society (and vice versa, of course) so well through the decades: the peregrine. Ironically, it was the legions of pigeon-fanciers – who sought to persecute the peregrine for its tendency to eat those most preposterous objects of any thinking mammal's affections, and petitioned the Home Office to remove legal protection from the species – who were its ultimate saviours.

In response to the petition, a Peregrine Inquiry was launched in 1960 by the Nature Conservancy, as it was then, and the British Trust for Ornithology: the results showed that British peregrine populations had declined to less than half of average levels during the 1930s. Even the homing pigeon set was sufficiently impressed by those findings to drop the matter.

There followed an extraordinary scientific detective story, in which data collected and presented by the Society, among others, on numerous species, figured prominently. Data on relative thicknesses of eggshells contributed to an absorbing sub-plot in which the DDT group of poisons was also implicated. By the mid-seventies the ban on both groups was more or less complete, although pesticides of all kinds remain a problem to this day.

Pesticides are among the more alarming of the various chemicals deliberately or accidentally introduced into the environment; but the list of substances that must be the object of continuing conservationist vigilance is itself never-ending. Since the mid-seventies, for example, the Society has been struggling, with various degrees of success, to alert the public to chemical threats to the Norfolk Broads, England's largest freshwater wetland areas left over from the peat-diggings of our medieval ancestors.

There are more than 40 broads, ranging from narrow navigation channels to the National Nature Reserve of Hickling Broad with an open water area of no less than 320 acres. All are shallow, less than six feet deep, and together form a deliciously mucky habitat of the sort in which certain life-forms, as I have celebrated elsewhere in this book, welter revoltingly and flourish. Trouble in paradise here takes the form of disturbance by holiday visitors, botulism in the stagnant waters, and above all a phenomenon known in its extreme form as eutrophication, which means simply the unnaturally vigorous growth of certain bacteria and plants, mainly algae, until they dominate the habitat.

Effluents from sewage works and run-off from farmland, carrying excessive nutrients in the forms of nitrates and phosphates, on which the undesirable species thrive, are the cause of much eutrophication, and in this case most of it. Farm fertilisers and wastes are almost impossible to control fully without the kind of government commitment that can be very dangerous politically; and although the conservationist (as opposed to agricultural) view has come to be taken more seriously of late, it may yet be necessary to 'write off' some of the larger public broads, concentrate on smaller and more easily managed areas, or even create new ones custom-made for habitat conservation.

The Broads are a good example of an area whose conservation combines issues of pollution and habitat mismanagement on an almost unimaginably large scale. Another such area is the uplands of Britain, the north of Scotland in particular, where many critics of government afforestation policies argue that those policies are themselves a kind of pollution, supplanting invaluable moorland with monocultures of conifers that support far fewer species, destroying landscapes of breathtaking visual beauty in the process. Even in lowland Britain, the relics of our native hardwood forest are threatened with clearance, if not for yet another monotonous stand of 'foreign' spruce and pine then for agricultural use. The Society, predictably, takes a dim view of all this; and a preoccupation with forestry issues could easily last the century out.

In terms of individual bird species, there are few that have not been affected in some adverse way by pollution, however narrowly defined. Dippers, which breed alongside streams and rivers throughout northern and western Britain, have been shown to be sensitive to acidification of water courses because they are so dependent on a diet of invertebrates; indeed, research by the Society (among others) suggests that declines in dipper populations may be among the most reliable indicators that a catchment area has fallen victim to 'acid rain'. The 14 species of raptor (birds of prey) breeding in Britain are still recovering in various degrees from the disastrous effects of agricultural chemicals earlier this century – sparrowhawks and peregrines, for example, are well on the increase again, while carrion-eaters such as the buzzard, which during the worst decades suffered reproductive damage from the most improbable sources, such as residues of dieldrin sheepdip, are somewhat less of a success story. (Declines in barn

The mute swan; a familiar sight on many waterways, but no longer common on some rivers that are heavily fished. Fishing line and discarded tackle provide dramatic hazards – more insidious is lead poisoning The swans pick up fishermen's split shot weights from riverbanks, when eating the grit they need for digestion.

The Young Ornithologists' Club has organised riverside walks to collect discarded fishing tackle. The RSPB set up, in co-operation with the National Federation of Anglers, a campaign of public education, advocating the use of alternatives to lead weights, and a booklet Anglers' Choice was produced. Legislation prohibiting the sale of lead weights was passed in 1987.

owl populations, however, increasingly seem only marginally related to pollution or poisoning, and more probably to the virtual disappearance in many areas of the agricultural settlements and buildings in which they used to nest, a development taken into account by recent campaigns, by the Society and others.)

The deliberate (and illegal) misuse of poisons against birds of prey on estates managed for game and on upland sheep farms has been the focus of one of the Society's more vigorous campaigns during the eighties.

The total of confirmed incidents of deliberate poisoning is small, 311 between 1966 and 1978. Altogether 53 species of bird and six species of mammal were recorded as victims of the misuse of poisons; but eight of those bird species were rare or threatened, and 26 in all specially protected by law. "Poisoning has the most serious implications on the scarcer species of birds of prey such as the red kite", the Society concluded in 1980. "Recruitment in such small populations may be insufficient to make good losses from persecution." Buzzards and golden eagles may be especially at risk, and poisoning (or shooting) is thought to be the likeliest reason for their continued scarcity in some areas despite the survival of apparently suitable habitats.

When thinking about pollution it is important to remember two somewhat contradictory principles: that pollution control is one of the few aspects of conservation which it is relatively easy to do something about by legislation, but that the persistence of pollution is the result of an abiding flaw in what can only be termed the character of the species. Men, women and children are, not to put too fine a point on it, slobs. They are born slobs, they mature as slobs and they die slobs. The development of pollution as an issue in domestic and international politics this century has been a sorry tale of as little as possible, as late as possible, and history repeating itself obsessively even unto the final chapter.

Oiled guillemots recuperating at the RSPCA centre at Little Creech.

120

8. Cops & robbers

Peter Robinson follows his own calendar. He writes,

> "To a large extent our work is seasonal, with deliberate poisoning commencing in the early spring, soon to be followed by egg collecting and then thefts of young birds of prey as the eggs hatch. There is a slight resurgence of poisoning around mid-summer, accompanied by an increase in the use of pole traps, both of which coincide with the introduction of young artificially reared pheasants into the release pens; the build up of the autumn post-breeding finch flocks then brings the bird trapper into his own and by late autumn wildfowling is in full swing and the cowboy element are making themselves conspicuous. Taxidermy and import and export cases are dealt with according to necessity."

Mr Robinson is the RSPB's senior investigations officer, in effect its chief constable. It is he who organises the involvement of the Society in the efforts of law-enforcement agencies to distinguish a red-capped from a pileated parrot, a poisoned kestrel from a stuffed passenger pigeon, an illegally imported hummingbird from your common or garden variety budgerigar. These comparisons are not entirely facetious: of the 150,000 or so police officers in the UK, there cannot be more than a dozen – there may be none at all – capable of making the first distinction, and there are probably many scores of thousands who would have trouble with the others.

Bird protection, furthermore, is unlikely to rank very high on the average policeman's list of priorities. The uniformed beat officer, as Robinson puts it,

> "tends to spend most of his time in the areas of highest human concentration, often seeing most of his 'wildlife' on Saturday evening when the public houses turn out, or during home team football matches. As for the plainclothesmen, their interpretation of what does and does not constitute a crime generally works against the likelihood of their becoming involved in a wildlife-related offence.
>
> "This is unfortunate because the people who exploit our wildlife most and whose activities have the greatest effect on the environment are only likely to be brought before the courts through the employment of skills and abilities peculiar to the criminal investigations officer."

By 1968, when the RSPB's Council decided to appoint a full time enforcement officer, it had become apparent that the triumphant passage of the Protection of Birds Act, 1954, generated almost as many problems as it solved. For one thing, enactment at last

Ian Prestt

An institution that prospers becomes an irresistible target for criticism. We British tend to look askance at success in any case (although we are not exactly enamoured of the failures in our midst either), and there is something soft and tempting about bureaucracy in particular that brings out the bully in us. The Society is no exception; the retirement of Peter Conder in 1975 inspired a fine example of such institution-bashing. John Hillaby, the man who walks around for a living, took the opportunity to criticise the Society's "arrogance in believing it has the right to play at God": in particular, the poisoning of gulls' eggs in order to enable other species to flourish, and the barring of some reserves to visitors.

But Hillaby had the good grace to admit that a chat with Ian Prestt, Mr Conder's successor, had changed his mind. "I am obliged to report that, in the non-equivocal manner of a Northerner, he promptly pruned some of the branches of my gripe vine. . . ." The new director, Hillaby said, was "a naturalist with a scientific training and government background", who might be the man to "transform what I've often been tempted to regard as an army without a clear idea of what it's up against". In short, the writer concluded: "He is intent on creating an army of informed naturalists."

Hillaby was wrong about Mr Conder, and it was a shame that a friendship of some years' standing should have ended in sarcasm and rancor, all because of what was seen, in the words of the object of all this veiled opprobium, as "a lack of fire in my belly". But Hillaby was right about Mr Prestt, who celebrates his 60th birthday in the Society's centenary year.

He came to the directorship of the Society when he was 46, an age when many other men might have been thinking in terms of a quiet backwater. He brought to the job not only the vigour more typical of a much younger man, but also 20 years' experience in conservation work: in the Nature Conservancy, as ornithological officer for Great Britain and with the toxic chemical and wildlife research team studying effects of pesticides and pollutants on Britain's birds; in the Central Unit on Environmental Pollution in the Cabinet Office, later incorporated in the Department of the Environment, and then as deputy director of the Nature Conservancy Council.

Under his directorship, the society has seen the acquisition of its hundredth reserve, the Wood of Cree; steady but not unreasonable growth in the various bureaucratic instruments necessary to the livelihood of an institution; consistent increases in membership and in financial turnover, and perhaps most importantly, significant participation by the Society in a majestic series of national and international safeguards to wildlife and their habitats, from the Endangered Species (Import/Export) Act 1976, through the EEC Birds Directive in 1979 and on to the Wildlife and Countryside Acts, 1981 and 1985. In 1986 Mr Prestt was awarded the CBE.

of reasonably comprehensive and effective legislation was bound to mean an increase in the numbers of prosecutions; for another, the explosive growth in membership meant that many more people turned to the Society as first resort when an offence was suspected. Members would call the Society for guidance and would be referred to the police – who would call the Society right back and ask them what to do next. Robinson, who has had the good sense to write a book about his experiences, was appointed to the post in 1974, and in so doing abandoned a career with the London Fire Brigade. He travels about 30,000 miles a year, and is in court four or five times a month. The department staff of seven deals with about 1,500 reports of offences, of which perhaps 100 are followed up and 50 will result in prosecutions, whether brought by the Society or by the police with the Society acting as advisers. The Scottish legal system discourages private prosecutions; although an enforcement officer works from the Edinburgh office to reasonable effect, the total numbers of prosecutions are therefore lower than might be expected.

Rarely, notes Robinson, do he or his colleagues ever come close to a nest site; and

> "we are unlikely to be involved in chasing people over wild hillsides . . . instead our work takes us to far less scenic localities, like Birmingham, Sunderland, Manchester or London's East End".

But the media do not share his view; to the average reporter the Society's enforcement work is the stuff of pure television, somewhere between *The Sweeney* and *All Creatures Great and Small*. That understandable preoccupation with the cops-and-robbers aspect of the Society's work has its unfortunate side-effects – an occasional tendency on the part of the public to see the Society as an animal welfare organisation, or to confuse it with the RSPCA – but it has its positive aspects as well. A good cops-and-robbers story sells newspapers; and a good newspaper story sells the Society. A member recruited through misunderstanding, joining the RSPB because he wants all egg-collectors shot and their children taken into care, is unlikely to do any harm, and might even learn a thing or two.

The Society has learned well the art of deploring publicity that it considers wide of the mark or inappropriate, while milking that publicity for all it is worth. However insignificant it may be in terms of the Society's overall activities, the enforcement side virtually guarantees a local column inch or two when a case comes to court, and often as not a mention in the national press too. Such statistics compare all too favourably with the media space and time devoted to the average press release deploring yet another plantation of conifers, or the threat, some generations hence as a rule, to yet another estuary somewhere in the back of beyond.

Wilson lives, or lived, in the north of England. From around the mid 1970s onwards we received reports of his car being seen parked at various places in Scotland or Wales during the summer months. On one occasion we heard that it had been seen at a group of small lochans holding breeding red-throated divers. About the same time, I learned from a reliable source that Wilson had been involved in the sale of an egg collecting cabinet and that the contents of the cabinet had formed part of the transaction. To put it another way, Wilson had sold the eggs of wild birds contrary to Section 6(1)(b) of the Protection of Birds Act 1954. I also learned that he had very recently returned from Scotland, bringing with him golden eagle eggs taken earlier that year.

At that time, I was fortunate in having Stuart Housden as my assistant. We discussed the developments in my office at Sandy, and agreed that, given other information we had about Wilson, we had sufficient evidence on which to proceed. We also agreed on the need to act swiftly lest the eggs move premises yet again. Breakfast time on 28th June saw Stuart and me far up the A1 trunk road on our way north. We arrived in time for a quick lunch before the Magistrates' Court resumed sitting and by 3 pm I had sworn the information for a search warrant and we had gone on to the police station – search warrants are granted if a magistrate is satisfied that eggs may have been sold illegally, but not if mere possession is alleged.

I discovered long ago the folly of descending upon a police station unannounced, and I had taken the precaution of telephoning the previous afternoon. The duty inspector was in the station and showed genuine interest in our little problem. Two plain-clothes officers were assigned to the execution of the warrant. We agreed to meet near the house at 5 pm, giving us a greater chance of finding someone in. This is always an important point to consider as ringing the doorbells of unattended houses can so easily result in a wasted search warrant, with neighbours saying, "The police were here while you were out. What have you been up to?"

The house was a typical two-storey, three-bedroom family house. Wilson's wife answered the door. It appeared that her husband was away in Scotland working on a contract job. She was shown the warrant and the police officers explained the circumstances briefly. She was not pleased to see us and made her feelings very clear, but she opened the door wide and invited us to search the house.

"Do you have any eggs in the house?" I asked her. "To save us causing too much disruption?"

"He has given up and got rid of his collection but we do have a few left." I asked if we could see them and she led us upstairs to the main bedroom. From on top of the wardrobe she took down a wooden box and threw back the lid, revealing about forty eggs of various common birds. They were all single eggs and they looked very like the sort of thing a schoolboy might keep.

I got the impression she was trying to mislead us: Stuart and I had both noticed that when she had taken down the box she had moved aside a similar box which had

The wheeling excitement of waders, bar-tailed godwit and knot, draw birdwatchers to estuaries. The UK has about 100 estuaries providing vital feeding grounds for some 1½ million waders and wildfowl.

In 1969, the RSPB produced a report on Foulness (Maplin) threatened by London's third airport. In 1978, RSPB members rallied to the defence of the Ribble Estuary, subsequently saved by the Government from development. But other estuaries are threatened by barrages, industry, ports, marines, recreation, even refuse tips. The RSPB launched a public awareness campaign about estuaries in 1987, and a film, Mud Matters, *in 1988.*

been on top of it. This second box was made of oak and measured about 18 inches square by 4 inches high.

"Can't you contact your husband?" I asked. Out of the corner of my eye I saw Stuart reach up and lift down the second box. He placed it on the double bed and went to open the lid but it was tighter than he had anticipated. A sudden change came over Wilson's wife as she took hold of the box.

"I'll show you what's in it," she exclaimed as she wrenched open the lid and tossed it back on the bed. She was very excited now and close to tears.

The interior of the box was divided into a number of compartments, each one full of cotton wool. She started flinging this out on to the bed, revealing that the box contained eggs. I was familiar with boxes of this type – they are often used by egg collectors for the transport and temporary storage of eggs.

"What are the four big ones?"

I felt like the actor in a Shakespearian play who is about to deliver a famous line.

"Those," I said, addressing myself to the officer who had asked the question, "are golden eagle eggs." The pigment markings on the four eagle eggs left Stuart and me in little doubt that they were from two clutches of two. One pair in particular were fine specimens, large even for eagle eggs, and identically covered with beautiful pink spots and blotches. All four eggs had writing on them.

A search of the room revealed a third wooden box containing some owl eggs and a plastic filing box of completed data cards, of the kind egg collectors keep to record the history of their trophies. We searched the remainder of the house methodically, including the roof space, until only the lounge remained. In the bottom of the book-case were 74 Ordnance Survey maps, some letters and a number of ruled foolscap textbooks. The maps were profusely marked with the nest sites of rare birds, particularly in the Scottish Highlands and around the red kite nesting area of Wales.

It was easy to see that Wilson had systematically searched the ornithological literature, gleaning information here and there that might pinpoint a nest site. His collection of books reflected the homework that he had done and in one of his notebooks was a list of published ornithological papers he intended to acquire.

Also in the notebooks were large scale detailed maps of red kite, golden eagle, peregrine falcon and diver nest sites, painstakingly drawn freehand. One of these happened to be an area on the west coast of Scotland that I was familiar with; the nests of two pairs of eagles were shown on it, both very close to each others.

The search had taken far longer than I had anticipated and we had located a considerable amount of material, most of which needed to be studied carefully. The officers were nearly finished when one of them opened the door of the airing cupboard, which was situated in the lounge. At this point I made what was to prove an unfortunate decision: the police officer asked me if it was worth removing the considerable contents of the cupboard, and I, aware that Stuart and I would not be home until the early hours, decided to leave the cupboard intact.

We gathered up all the items that we were removing to the police station, taking great care that Wilson's wife saw the writing on the eagle eggs. I did not want it suggested at some later date that we had written on the eggs after we had taken them from the house. Two of the eggs were marked '263.97-', the other two '303.97.'. I knew exactly what this meant, but we had yet to prove it!

It may sound as if my little story has almost reached a successful conclusion, but, alas, this is far from being the case. The 1954 Act makes it an offence to take, sell or exchange eggs, but not to be in possession of them. Before we could consider court action, we had either to prove that Wilson had taken the eggs, or, if he had not taken them, to find out who had. Without doubt, Wilson's story would be that he was looking after the eggs for a friend!

It wasn't just a matter of our finding out who took the eggs, either. Protection of Birds Act offences are dealt with summarily, before a magistrate's court, and prosecutors are bound by the six month 'limitation of proceedings'. Put simply, this means that information of the offence and offender has to be laid before a magistrate within six months of the commission of the offence; we could not prosecute for any eggs taken in previous years, even if we could prove our case.

We studied the maps, books and papers back at the office. Wilson was certainly active, for there were 675 nest sites recorded on forty-four of the maps, nearly all of specifically protected birds. The notebooks, too, were most enlightening.

We turned our attentions next to tracing Wilson's movements that March as the writing on the four eggs showed they had been taken on 26th and 30th March that same year. Our first clue was a receipt from a small hotel not far away from the two west coast eagle pairs shown in the notebook. It was dated 24th March, a room for two in Wilson's name. As hotel receipts are normally made out at the time of departure it appeared that our man had stayed there on the night of the 23rd, and with a companion, too.

Next we looked at the ruled textbooks. Some were neatly written diaries, others just rough notebooks. In one of the latter was an entry describing how Wilson had arrived at a loch on the morning of "the 24th" and inspected an eagle nest on a nearby hill. Both the loch and the hill were named, it was one of the two sites I had recognised in his notebook map. In vivid detail Wilson described how after several failures he finally looked down into the nest to discover that it contained "a well-marked pair" of eggs. He then described how he had visited the second pair of eagles and after much searching finally flushed the incubating female from a single egg. The notes suggested that he left the area on the 26th or 27th. The two eggs coded as having been collected on 26th March were the same two that had originally impressed me by their fine colouring – surely they must be Wilson's "well-marked pair"!

Among a pile of letters we found one received from a fellow egg collector not long after Wilson had returned from his eagle trip. "Very pleased to hear how you got on in Scotland," it read, "and look forward to seeing them sometime, especially the well-marked set." Clearly envious of Wilson, he continued, "We didn't do as well but did manage C6 long-eared owl and a C3 peregrine (clutch of 6 eggs and clutch of 3 eggs) but no eagles. We spent six days up there. . . . Of the 19 (eagle) sites visited we found only eight nests, seven definitely not being used, the other one looked promising but the weather was far too bad to use a rope.'

Now that we were close to the answers we sought, yet another complication reared its head for the offence we appeared likely to prove was that of taking eggs contrary to Section 1(c) of the 1954 Act. Summary offences of this nature must be heard before a magistrate or sheriff for the area in which the offence was committed; in Wilson's case this was on the west coast of Scotland. Private prosecutions are not permitted in

Scotland and that being the case it was necessary for me to hand the matter over to the police. They in turn would pass it to the Procurator Fiscal, who acts as the public prosecutor in Scotland.

There were still one or two loose ends to tidy up and I hoped we could do this at the same time that we went to see the Scottish police. For one thing we needed to verify that the two eagle nests in question had held eggs that year and if possible I wanted to confirm that Wilson had been in the area. The drive up the M6 was even more tedious than usual. It was a Saturday and all the service stations were jammed with holiday families so I pushed on, not stopping for a meal until I was far into the hills. More than ten hours after leaving Sandy I parked the car beside a rushing stream and slept soundly until 7.00 the next morning.

I awoke to find the sun shining. A small herd of red deer were feeding close to the car and they bounded away as I went down to the stream for a wash in the tingling water. I spent three hours searching the wooded gulley for the nest that had held one egg on 26th March, but failed miserably. One thing was fairly certain though, there was no young eagle in a nest in the gulley or I would have expected to see some sign of the parent birds; but of course this did not prove they had failed to breed that year because of an egg collector.

At lunchtime I drove down to the hotel where Wilson had stayed and ordered a sandwich. I would have liked to look at the register but could not find it in any of the public parts of the hotel. I decided against making a direct approach to the proprietor just in case he was on personal terms with Wilson. If questions had to be asked it was better that the police do it – for one thing, they have authority to instruct the proprietor to produce the register.

That afternoon I went to the local police station and made a statement, handing over all my evidence to the police in the process.

Some days later Stuart had cause to go up to Scotland and he too made statements. While he was there he managed to locate the other nest and confirmed that it had been occupied that year and that it was now empty. He also found rope marks on the cliff top directly above the nest.

The police wasted no time in passing the case to the Fiscal who, having regard for the greater degree of corroboration required by Scottish law, asked Wilson's local police to interview him. Detective Constable McKay was to conduct the interview, appropriately enough, and I was allowed to be present. It was put to Wilson that he had taken golden eagle eggs in Scotland on 26th and 30th March and that in addition on both occasions he had disturbed incubating eagles contrary to Section 4 of the Protection of Birds Act 1967. He denied taking the eggs but admitted being at both nests and disturbing the birds. He claimed he could prove he had not taken the eggs and offered to produce a notebook from his car if we did not take possession of it. In the circumstances we felt obliged to agree and the book was duly produced. He turned to a page headed 24th March, assuring us that it referred to that year. Keeping a tight hold on the book to prevent us turning the page he allowed us to read what was written there. I recognised Wilson's writing. It confirmed that he had been at one of the sites on that day and had flushed the female off "two well-marked eggs". We asked to look at the entry for 26th but Wilson refused. We pointed out that all he had proved so far was that he had disturbed an eagle off its eggs on the 24th.

We asked again if he had taken the eggs on the 26th. No, he hadn't, he replied, but he admitted being present when they were taken. So that was it. The DC asked him if he had assisted in the theft.

"Yes, near enough", came the reply. Near enough was good enough!

We asked one more time to see over the page but again he declined, telling us that if we did we would see the name of the person who was with him. The DC asked about the two eggs taken on 30th March. Wilson claimed there had only been one egg on 26th and alleged that 'someone' went back on 30th and took the completed clutch of two. Presumably that someone was Wilson's companion of 26th. It did not of course account for why the eggs were in Wilson's house when we visited. He explained this away by saying that the two eggs had been sent to him for marking and repair.

The notebook he produced interested me. Had we found it during our search, it would undoubtedly have thrown a different light on the enquiry. I asked where the book had been when we searched the house. He smiled. "In the one place you did not search – at the back of the airing cupboard." The possibility that he was lying in order to save face could not be dismissed, but I was inclined to believe him. I cursed inwardly.

Wilson was summonsed for three offences of wilfully disturbing golden eagles at the nest contrary to Section 4 of the 1967 Act and for the theft of two eagle eggs on the 26th. The case was heard in the Sheriffs' Court later that year. He did not appear, but wrote to the court offering a plea of guilty. For each of the disturbance offences he was fined £50 plus a further £200 for taking the eggs, making a total of £350.

As it is not usual for costs to be awarded in Scottish courts, none of the Society's expenses were recovered. However, the Sheriff did make use of his powers of confiscature, the two eggs were handed to the police and the Society eventually took custody of the seventy-four maps. With Ordnance Survey maps then costing £1·15 each this was a significant penalty in itself, but no doubt the greatest loss to Wilson was the information they contained.

The most annoying part of the whole enquiry came right at the conclusion when we were obliged to return to Wilson all the eggs we could not show had been taken that year. Even more frustrating, however, was the fact that we had to return the sixty data cards with their information on the eggs in Wilson's still undetected collection!

"A Well Marked Pair" from *Bird Detective* by Peter Robinson: Elm Tree Books/Hamish Hamilton (1982).

Robert Dougall

Robert Dougall was one of the earliest manifestations of that curious phenomenon of the television age: the newsreader who becomes a celebrity simply because, evening in and evening out, like a marginally more animated mountain peak, he or she is there. But few mountain peaks merit the adoration accorded to Mr Dougall in his day, nor the description "unaffectedly warm, friendly and sincere".

Such were the words of Herbert Axell, writing in *Birds* magazine, after Mr Dougall, "senior BBC television newsreader and a keen amateur ornithologist", was elected President of the Society, of which he had been an active member for 20 years, in 1970.

(Mr Axell himself was no slouch in the 'unaffected warmth' stakes; and professionally, he was one of the Society's great wardens, largely responsible for the pioneering land-management successes at Minsmere and later for the export of the Society's expertise to such internationally acclaimed reserves as Coto Doñana in Spain and the Maltese Ghadira Pool. Like Mr Dougall, he was also awarded an MBE.)

The new president was said to be so modest as to believe himself out of place among "those paragons of ornithological virtue whose biographies appeared in 'Personalities' in the old *Bird Notes*"; but in fact he was

> "well qualified to join their ranks. Equally at home in the field with a warden or at social gatherings, Robert has strong, lucidly expressed feelings on the quality of the environment."

A perfect combination, then: the charge of glamour adhering to television the show-business medium, as static electricity crackles on the surface of the tube itself; a fair amount of genuinely charismatic personal appeal, plus a gifted amateur's knowledge of birds and of the much broader conservation issues which make it sensible to worry about birds at all . . . and coming at a time when the public was just beginning to digest the masses of new information about wildlife for which television had helped to create such an appetite in the first place. This best known of BBC voices was, of course, also an ideal narrator for two of the Society's wildlife films, and many too young to have seen him on television will easily recognise that voice from the commentaries they have heard him speak.

Mr Dougall was born in Croydon in 1913, and joined the BBC as an accountant, becoming an announcer in the Empire Service on his 21st birthday. (It is probably significant that he had attended Whitgift School, which had a very active Selborne Society.) He had a busy war, first as a news reporter and later with the RNVR at the naval base in the Russian Arctic. An excellent linguist, good enough to broadcast in French, German and Russian, he is a three-time winner of the Royal National Institute for the Deaf award as the clearest speaker on television, also raising scores of thousands of pounds on behalf of the Institute through television appeals.

Like so many others involved with the Society, Mr Dougall clearly cares at least as much for people as for birds. It is sometimes tempting to consider whether the do-gooding instinct might not be in some respects no less indiscriminate and insatiable than those it seeks, so often in vain, to counter.

133

A project set up with the government of Ghana and the International Council for Bird Preservation to prevent the destruction of seashore birds. Trapping terns is a favourite pastime for young boys along the coast. Particularly vulnerable are young roseate terns, Europe's rarest breeding tern.

135

Max Nicholson

Max Nicholson has been perhaps more widely honoured than many of the *dramatis personae* in these pages; but his is nonetheless anything but a household name. Such, sadly, is all too often the fate of environmentalists, however brilliant. My theory is it has something to do with the stupidity of news editors, most of whom may know a good environmental story – well, a *very*, very good environmental story – when they see one, but who lack the intellectual equipment to understand the scientific thinking behind the story, or even to recognise that thinking as scientific. This is changing, but too slowly to do the likes of Dr Nicholson much good.

His presidency of the Society, from 1980 to 1985, was inevitably something of a footnote to the long and fascinating life of a man whom *The Environmentalist* magazine in 1983 described as "one of the main catalysts and architects of the environmental movement". He was born in 1904, read history at Oxford, served with distinction in a variety of peacetime and wartime government jobs, and in 1952 became Director-General of the UK Nature Conservancy. "For the next 14 years", *The Environmentalist* notes, "he pioneered the development of conservation within government and in the non-governmental section, nationally and internationally. It will take many a doctoral thesis to evaluate his outstanding contribution during this time."

Of his contributions to ornithology in particular, Phyllis Barclay-Smith, writing in *Bird Notes* credits him with being among the first to develop the techniques of census-taking without which bird conservation would be unthinkable today; with inventing the idea of dividing the Atlantic into 10-degree squares in order to study the distribution of marine birds, and with a superb ear for birdsong.

He brought to the Society, in short, a unique perspective, incorporating technical and scientific genius and an intellectual sophistication that was not merely inter-national but – long before such concepts became catchphrases and the bases of lucrative, jet-setting careers – truly global.

Dr Nicholson himself attributes his achievements not to academic brilliance (his several doctorates are in fact honorary) but to an ability "to doze or daydream through enough of my school lessons to avoid the process of intellectual sterilisation inflicted upon my more wakeful colleagues".

9. Catching them young

The distinction is to some extent artificial, as the Society, like any organisation with an axe to grind, is by definition engaged in educational work whatever its activities. There must be the *a priori* assumption that the public is in some way ignorant, lacking in common sense; otherwise the well meaning people who have set out to change all that would stand bereft of arguments to support their case, do-gooders without a cause.

So enormously complicated are the implications of any conservationist issue, and so fundamentally blind to those implications any given element of the population, that it seems unlikely any group espousing any objective whatever concerning the environment would be unable to muster some support, somewhere for its ideals. Having said that, the objective is to get as much support as possible so as to outnumber the opposition, or at least be first past the post – opposition, very often including competing clusters of like-minded idealists no less than those whom all concerned in the crusade would unhesitatingly define as The Enemy.

That crusade, accordingly, is bound to be, if it is run intelligently in large measure a Children's Crusade. It is a process of brain-washing, conditioning, propaganda . . . call it what you will. The principle of childhood recruitment for future ideological ends can be and has been exploited, with relatively minor variations, for far more nefarious purposes than the Society would ever contemplate. But it is important to remember that the manipulation and indoctrination of children is a professional technique like any other, not always comparable to the fundamental and continuing process of adult education that is the lifeblood of any pressure group.

Any voluntary agency whose subject matter embraces natural history starts with an advantage: our conditioning in infancy to lavish indiscriminate affection on those cuddly animals which later in life we will annihilate with such insouciance. In building on that foundation, the tendency, curiously enough, is to ape the very institution, school, whose control of children tends to be based not on persuasion but on coercion. So: award schemes, classes, grades (at least in the sense of working one's way though a hierarchy of information if not always knowledge), projects of a practical nature – a selling point to any parent, surely, if only because such projects get the kids off their hands for at least as long as it takes to do them – and finally, it is hoped, a kind of 'graduation', in the Society's case, to fully fledged anorak, binoculars, and all-round ornithologically inclined adulthood.

Logically enough, a great deal of the Society's work with children is carried out through the school system. Sir Peter Scott has given his blessing to the process in laudatory (and mandatory) style:

The EEC Directive on the Conservation of Wild Birds came into force in 1981. It was largely modelled on existing British legislation, but by 1984 not one member state had adequately fulfilled its obligations and a number of countries faced infringement proceedings from the European Commission.

Bird trapping and shooting continue to concern the RSPB's international office, which together with the ICBP, launched in the UK the "Stop the Massacre Fund" to raise funds to support projects to prevent the annual slaughter of migratory birds in southern Europe.

(a) and (d) Children in Malta campaign against the illegal trapping of robins (1985).

(b) Hunters in Italy.

(c) An Italian hunter proudly displays his kill – a skylark (1976).

(e) RSPB staff travelled to France in 1974 to give support to French conservationists protesting about the trapping of small birds.

"Nothing is more important than teaching the next generation about the value to people of the natural world around us – a world that is so gravely threatened by human ignorance and apathy."

The first and most obvious step is of course to sell the idea to the adults who run the schools and whose charges must do more or less what they are told. Towards that end the Society runs a large and attractively bureaucratic Education Department with four regional officers, and a dozen staff, no fewer than half of whom are engaged in running the Young Ornithologists' Club, headquartered at The Lodge.

In its recruiting material for teachers, the Society claims that the Education Department "with strong justification . . . can claim to be a leader among the voluntary organisations in the promotion of public interest in conservation and the environment".

In-service courses are available for teachers – an enticingly different break, I should have thought, from the ghastly routine of a teacher's life – and a regular newsletter, *Focus on Birds*, keeps them up to date. In a typical year more than 4,000 teachers would attend about 1,500 weekend, day-long, multi-part or single session courses. Supplementary talks in various educational institutions would be aimed at further recruitment, especially of trainee teachers, while the voluminous flow of teaching literature (including the RSPB's own films and videos) is a further inducement to carry on availing oneself of an occasional speciality with the kind of support teachers in many other disciplines can only dream about.

Field trips to the most accessible of the seven reserves that also function as Nature Centres or 'Country Classrooms' are an attractive prospect for most children, and perhaps for their teachers too. And of course, when class is over and school is out, "for those children who become interested in birds and who wish to develop this further as a hobby, there is the Young Ornithologists' Club, the Junior Membership of the RSPB". Children up to the age of 16 can join as individuals, under family membership, or in a school group as such. At last count there were about 2,000 school groups; young ornithologists altogether totalled almost 90,000.

The importance of 'education' in its specialised sense – that is, of involving children in the activities of the Society – seems to have been recognised at a remarkably early stage. By 1904, the year of its incorporation by Royal Charter, when the Society itself was barely pubescent, 1,200 elementary schools were already enlisted in a '*Bird and Tree*' scheme, which had started as a campaign, unsuccessful in the event, to establish a Bird and Tree Day in the British Isles, with essay-writing contests, awards ceremonies, and all the paraphernalia of spurious competition, which all children are supposed to love but which in fact are universally detested, except by the winners, who tend (in 'education' as in real life) to be the same small group of thugs, bullies and lickspittles.

Hudson, whom I sincerely trust was none of these, is said to have taken a great interest in the Bird and Tree competition from its inception in 1902. Ultimately the object of the exercise was simply to write the best essay describing a bird or tree that had been studied. Winners received regional plaques and the loathing of their less successful peers. Their modern equivalents are more likely to turn up in the pages of *Bird Life*, the magazine of the YOC, a fine-looking publication that often absorbs the

For many years the Bird and Tree competition was the Society's principle attempt at encouraging an interest in birds and wildlife among children. Here Sir Peter Scott presents the Bird and Tree shield to the winning school. Now the Young Ornithologists' Club promotes several awards and activities, like its Action for Birds Awards and Young Ornithologist of the Year, together with fun days and a nationwide network of local groups.

attention of adults, and not infrequently is rather more amusing than the grown-up *Birds.* Other educational publications as such include the various project guides, models of clarity all, easily understandable even by teachers.

It is not entirely clear whether YOC members grow up in any appreciable quantity to be adult birdlovers, members of the Society, or simply devoted husbands and wives, mothers and fathers, and conscientious payers of bills and voters in elections. But the philosophy of education is and has ever been that something, somehow must stick, and it seems unlikely that hours of childhood spent watching birds can cause any harm. At the very least it gets the little brutes out in the fresh air and away from the video nasties – and its publicity value for the Society as a whole is incalculable.

Visitors to The Lodge can walk through the formal gardens that surround the building. Built in 1870 in Victorian Tudor style, the house was designed by Henry Clutton for Arthur Wellesley Peel. In 1934, The Lodge was purchased by Sir Malcolm Stewart. The picture above shows a view of the front of the house taken in 1938.

10. International relations

Conventions, protocols, all that sort of thing. They are landmarks in a world that I have always suspected does not exist. It is the world of the KGB (or of Smersh), of the CIA (or James Bond); in the UK, whose fantasies, like most things about it, are rather more complex than other nations, we have MI5 and 6 and *Tinker Tailor* and *Smiley's People* and newspaper stories about books about spies that nobody really understands. People retire in disgrace, or go to jail, or defect even . . . and yet none of these things really exist, I say, except as an industry to keep people like me (only much more clever) in business. What the spies have in common with transnational cross-speak about birds and the like is that they inhabit a no-place of the mind, a limbo if not a purgatory, where perceptions blur to the point of purblindness.

Environment generally is a bit like that, too. One deals in principles, causes and consequences so general, so vast and incomprehensible, or so minute and immeasurable, and always so speculative, that almost anything can be said with confidence that it is more likely than not to be true. I have always had difficulty explaining to Scandinavian friends, for example, that I do not 'believe in' acid rain: I only write about it sometimes, or what people say about it, or what it feels like to be out in some dreadful sopping-wet forest looking for the stuff. Similarly, returns are far from in on the environmental effects attributable to the accident at the Chernobyl nuclear power station in 1986, and even when they are they will be little more than a collection of interpretations looking for experts to adopt them. There will be no consensus – in environment, there never is.

When we think about environment, then, one of the many things we are trying to come to grips with is the notion of borders. Real borders in imaginary landscapes; or perhaps it is the other way around. Consider the no-man's-land we have all crossed at one time or another, between the frontier of one country and another. The point where France ends is different from the line where Belgium, or whatever, begins. There is something in between: you can see it, you can measure it. But what is it? *Where* is it? What is its name? Who are you when you stand upon it? Who owns treasure that may be found on that land? There are laws, you will answer – there must be – to settle just such controversies. Of course. But who understands them, where do you find out about them; is there anything about them recognisable to us as logic?

We have already seen in a previous chapter how even domestic wildlife law relating to birds is such a closed book to the local PC Plod that a registered charity ends up doing the policing most of the time, if it gets done at all. International law, such as it is, is even worse. It scrambles the brains even of those who are paid to create it, and if you don't believe me try holding a coherent conversation – about anything – with an international bureaucrat sometime. (If you happen to be in Geneva and can't find a UN type around, give the World Wildlife Fund, or better, the International Union for Conservation of Nature and Natural Resources, a ring. Closer to home, there are a few lesser examples of the breed right here at The Lodge.) They talk all right; fluently and at great length. But information is not what they are purveying.

There is a distinction between 'hard' and 'soft' law, which students of juris-prudence, at least, find useful. Roughly speaking, hard law carries a penalty for failure to observe it, and soft law is merely an expression of good intentions, all spirit, as it were, and no letter. By and large, international conventions tend towards the soft, and even where there are provisions enabling signatory governments to write them into the law of the land, they tend to languish in obscurity. I once called the Department of the Environment and asked who was responsible for enforcing the estimable Convention on International Trade in Endangered Species of Wild Fauna and Flora (or 'CITES', pronounced 'Sigh-tease'). Nobody knew. Customs & Excise told me they thought it might be Uxbridge Police Station, though they couldn't swear to it. The duty officer at Uxbridge thought I was a practical joker.

Now CITES is serious business. It tells you which plants and animals, and which products deriving from them, you are allowed to take across a border, and which you are not. It names those species, sets them up in categories and lists, and tries to make it easy as possible for the participating nations to use them. Every so often some of the best minds in the field meet for some weeks to update, refine and strengthen the convention. It can fine you or send you to jail. It is not, strictly speaking, 'soft law'; but it is typical in its near cosmic importance on the one hand, vitiated on the other by its recondite technicality, its elusiveness, its ultimate remoteness and impenetrability.

Mrs Lemon has chronicled the quixotic battle against international oil pollution, which included the foundation of the International Council for Bird Preservation. The ICBP was created in 1922 in order to facilitate co-operation among the various voluntary groups, with each country represented by a national section. "It is interesting to note," writes Bassett, "that in other fields of wildlife preservation international liaison rarely developed before the late 1940s." Last time I visited the headquarters of the ICBP, the staff were working in and sharing a collection of draughty Portakabins in Cambridge with a scruffy team of underpaid scientists who catalogue endangered species for the so-called Red Data Books, which nowadays of course more closely resemble 'Red Data Discs' . . . all adding up to not only yet another indigestible string of initials, but also a paradigm of modesty belying the importance of the work they are doing.

At one point, however, the RSPB's loss proved to be the ICBP's gain: Phyllis Barclay-Smith was a relatively modern version of the Society's breed of 'formidable women'. When she resigned as assistant secretary to the RSPB, another of Mrs Lemon's victims (see Chapter 2), she devoted her attentions and energy to ICBP, dominating it virtually from her arrival in 1935 until her death, aged 77, in 1980. During her previous incarnation with the RSPB she was thought to have been the first member of staff to write a scientific paper and, according to her obituarist, Dr W R P Bourne,

"she eventually received more national and international awards than all the rest put together, so that it would take a page to list them. No meeting was complete until she had been given one.

145

For love of birds: the story of the RSPB

"The daughter of a professor of anatomy, she was well educated but apparently not academically distinguished, a late-developer. She became assistant secretary or stooge to the RSPB under the old regime in 1924 and created a sensation with an oration about oil pollution to the Seventh International Ornithological Congress at Amsterdam in 1930."

She became Secretary-General of the ICBP in 1946 and just a few years before her death, Vice-President, and had been involved in setting up (among other things) the International Wildfowl Research Bureau and the Advisory Committee on Oil Pollution of the Sea. Like so many of the great and good and little-known,

"she worked in a back room at the Natural History Museum and her influence spread far and wide among the national and international conservation establishment, who loved her and loaded her with honours".

We have seen, as we probably felt instinctively in the first place, how any obsession with birds was perforce a transboundary affair: birds migrate, and even if they do not it is all too easy, perfectly natural in fact, for a bird to fly across a border, on one side of which it will be cherished and on the other shot and eaten. Importation of birds, prominently among other things, was what inspired the formation of the Society.

In recent years, CITES has been the foundation of some of the Society's most important work. Two modern studies of the importation of birds into the UK, published in the mid-seventies and based on the work that is the meat of the convention, raised disquieting echoes of the earliest campaigns. Peter Conder, in writing his introduction to the first report, *All Heaven in a Rage* (a title which used the same quotation from William Blake as Turner's classic*), could not have been unconscious of Victorian literary precedent when he wrote in his introduction:

"It is even more sobering to ask oneself how many birds are originally caught to provide the 600,000 imported into Britain every year. Many are trapped by the local people with the aid of liming and other barbarous techniques, and kept in atrocious crowded conditions. How many of these die before they reach the exporter? Perhaps 50%, or 75%, or even more? Many of the catchers and exporters regard the colourful birds as the most valuable; indeed, we know that they do not always bother to send off the dull-coloured females and immatures, which are therefore torn from the lime-sticks and left to die. To what figure does this bring the percentage mortality? A conservative estimate of the world trade is five million birds per year, but this figure may well be 10 million or 25 million and how many birds are caught to produce this? 100 million? Or more?"

The second report, *Airborne Birds*, noted that the Government had "acted with commendable speed" in response to the challenge set by the Society, but that loopholes remained, especially in the enforcement of regulations drawn up by the airlines themselves. This report had a distinct air of tying up loose ends while further exploiting publicity generated by the first, suggesting perhaps that a campaign too

*A Robin Red breast in a Cage
Puts all Heaven in a Rage
      (*Auguries of Innocence*)

easily won is less useful in some ways than one which is encouraged to founder a bit in controversy. In fact, and entirely by coincidence, MAFF ultimately did the right thing for the wrong reasons: an outbreak of Newcastle disease in poultry brought about restrictions on bird importation strict enough to soothe the savage breast of the most impassioned conservationist.

A rather more amusing initiative concerned what is thought to have been the first independently contrived international agreement between the sovereign government of one nation and voluntary agencies representing another. In 1985, the government of Ghana and the Society, with the International Council for Bird Preservation, signed a memorandum of agreement to work for the conservation of seashore birds and their Ghanaian habitat, whence many migratory species of importance to the British, in particular the roseate tern, tend to winter. Trapping the hapless birds had become a popular pastime for boys along the coast, and the 'Save the Seashore Birds Project – Ghana' had the virtue of enabling the Ghanaian authorities to take the first step towards controlling the slaughter.

The seashore birds project is a fine example of international work that may not eventuate in legislation, at least not in this country. But it augurs well for the future activities of the Society's international office, which otherwise is bound to spend much of its time (when not engaged in the kind of liaison work natural to any body of enthusiasts with vast numbers of friends and colleagues abroad, in ceremonial affairs of a global nature), lobbying in the court of public opinion overseas as the main body of the Society lobbies at home, but to less immediately obvious effect.

One exception is the European Community, where the influence of the Society (among others, as usual, and most especially the ICBP) has been evident in legislation affecting birds and the environment directly or otherwise. Within the mind-boggling bureaucracy of Europe indomitable bands of the converted struggle constantly to inject an element of conservation into deliberations that can all too easily work unintended havoc on the environment, as the world has only recently begun to appreciate with the notorious Common Agricultural Policy. But even in this relatively hospitable arena, it was only in 1986-87, a generation after the Treaty of Rome, that the first ponderous steps were taken to make environmental considerations mandatory in EEC legislation.

The international office of the Society is considered important enough, notwithstanding its public near-invisibility, that it works directly to the office of the Director General.

11. The Lodge: the RSPB today

I am gazing at a chart on which are depicted 'RSPB staff relationships and main functions'. It is a dispiriting sight. There are more than forty little boxes, each with the name of a department, or individual, or both; to an outsider it makes about as much sense as its equivalents issued by, say, ICI, RTZ, the Foreign & Commonwealth Office, or any of those corporations, institutions or bureaucracies which take themselves rather too seriously. We all know who and what they are, and we all know that they have nothing to do with us.

What ever happened to that brave little band of 'formidable women'? What would Mrs Lemon think about her baby now? How would she interpret those little boxes marked 'Cons Div Liaison' and 'Hd Land Agent/Prin Reserves Officer', not to mention 'Data Processing' (underneath, graphically speaking, but no immediate relation to, 'Accounts Mail Opening/Cashiers')? Such, as I have remarked more than once, is the price of progress. Nobody likes it. And yet it is no small part of that which I have been commissioned to celebrate in this volume.

I have read somewhere that an organisational removal of a corporate headquarters is equivalent, in its disruptive effects and loss of productivity, to a third of a fire. The Lodge was the exception, and to this day it remains not only a most imposing symbol of a corporate success story, but also a mitigation of the unappetising bureaucracy which it has nurtured. For one thing, it is a nice place, and people who work there tend to like it; for another, its grounds are themselves a reserve, so that the product, as it were, is always visible, even to those toiling away in the bowels of (more little boxes) 'Appeals and Funding', 'Membership Registry', or for that matter 'Con Plan'.

The role of businesses generally in saving old buildings which no individual could these days afford to buy or maintain is vastly underappreciated. It is yet another aspect of convergence, and one which also gives public pleasure irrespective of its practical benefits. Property can also be a wonderful way for a voluntary organisation to make money – just like any other property owner. The leasehold of Eccleston Square was sold in 1961 for £67,500, exactly 10 times its cost eight years earlier. The Lodge that year was, to put it mildly, a snip at £25,000.

Literature published by the Society about its headquarters is rather surprisingly sparse, and apt to dispense with the bureaucratic and historical side of The Lodge in fairly short order. Here is what one brochure says.

> "The Lodge, the headquarters of the RSPB since 1961, stands in 104 acres, one mile to the east of the A1 and one-and-a-half miles south-east of Sandy on part of an outcrop of Lower Greensand known as Sandy Warren.

148

Table 2 RSPB membership growth from 1945-1987		
Year	No of members	No of YOC members
1945	5,869	
1950	6,265	
1955	7,004	
1960	10,579	
1965	29,719	
1970	66,807	34,986
1975	206,241	68,000
1980	321,391	100.000
1985	390,000	85,000*
1987	440,000	100,000
*Fall reflected lowered birth-rate during 1970s.		

With an annual "drop-out" of approximately 7%, the Society now has to recruit 30,000 members each year just to "stand still". Once members have joined for two or three years, they tend to stay loyal to the Society.

Built in 1870, the house, which was originally a private residence, is a good example of the Victorian Tudor style. It was designed by Henry Clutton for Arthur Wellesley Peel, the youngest son of the famous statesman, Robert Peel. In 1862 Arthur Peel married Adelaide, daughter of Sir William Dugdale, and the armorial bearings over the front porch are those of the two families. Arthur Peel was Speaker of the House of Commons from 1884 to 1895, when he was the first Viscount Peel of Sandy.

In 1934, The Lodge was purchased by Sir Malcolm Stewart, and many improvements to the house and gardens were carried out, including the building of the swimming pool, now a fish pond, on the lawn.

The RSPB bought The Lodge and moved its headquarters from London in 1961. Since then, the surrounding 104 acres have been managed in consultation with the Bedfordshire and Huntingdonshire Naturalists' Trust as a nature reserve."

End of introduction, end of extraneous material. The remaining 15 pages of the brochure are devoted to the natural history and management of The Lodge as a reserve, including a list of about 150 species recorded on or over the reserve. The anonymous authors are to be commended for their healthy sense of priorities.

But such a property will inevitably have acquired a history of general interest, even to the least ornithologically inclined. The editor of this book, for example, had family in service at The Lodge, a gratifying instance of generational continuity no less than of upward mobility. Not long ago, an elderly gentleman wrote from retirement in Brighton to cast a much different but equally benign anecdotal light upon The Lodge.

S A Charlwood was, he said,

"a member who started to take an interest in birdwatching rather late in life, as I am now about 70 years old. How I wish that the interest had been generated in my youth, as I realise the pleasure and opportunity I have missed.

"Ten years ago when I first became interested my attention was drawn to the RSPB. On some literature I had I saw the address of Headquarters shown as The

Lodge, Sandy, Bedfordshire, and this aroused much more interest. Why? you may wonder. I decided I must have a look at this and see for myself what it was like as a bird reserve. Accordingly, in the summer of 1977 I booked into a hotel in Sandy that I had seen advertised in *Birds*.

"The next day I made my way to The Lodge to have a look round. I found it much as I expected, but then this was not my first visit. The first visit was on 26th May 1941 and the purpose of this letter is to record a bit of history of the site that may or may not be known. In 1941 the woods around The Lodge were part of 84 Command Ammunition Depot to which I had just been posted. Lining the drive approaching The Lodge from main road were iron shelters containing stacks of high explosive shells. The woods on either side were fitted with shelters containing various types of ammunition. On the right hand side of the drive as you enter from the main road there was a narrow gauge railway winding away through the trees, and the gap is still there where the track was laid. The 'Strictly No Admission' notices were not there – there was a guard instead. The public right of way was closed. The area in the hollow round 'Jacks Hide' was used for the storage of shells containing poisonous gas, and on my holiday visit I remembered the many trips I made to the site as an Ammunition Examiner to check for safety.

"I did see some signs of the old brickwork that formed the base of the road – now the public right of way – leading off the main drive, and which was rubble from bombed buildings in London. This point was the nearest the depot approached The Lodge, and the resident was Sir Malcolm Stewart, chairman of the London Brick Company."

Meanwhile, back at The Lodge, the phones as usual are ringing. The telephonists have developed, perforce, that chirpy, friendly but impersonal edge that we tend to consider, mistakenly, an exclusively American vice. It is not their fault, and at least they manage not to sound as harassed as they indubitably are.

More than 10,000 people ring up during the course of a year, and another 5,000 or so write, with questions about birds, what they are, what to do with them or about them. The volume intensifies in cold weather, when worrying about our birdlife is as traditional as complaining about a climate that is, in fact, enviably temperate by almost any standards. Most such calls, which come on top of the enormous telephone traffic required to run one of the largest conservation businesses in the world, are referred to and answered by information officers in the library, which is itself something of a resource, with thousands of volumes by no means exclusively dealing with birds in general or the Society in particular, but adding up to a surprisingly well balanced environmental collection, irrespective of the Society's own historical archives.

With a permanent staff of more than 400, most of them working from The Lodge, and a gross annual income of about £9 million, the Society operates as any fair-sized business, albeit in the unlikely setting of this Victorian mansion. As a business, it organises its functions into four main categories: reserves, conservation, information and education, and sales and fund-raising, whence spring the various boxes on the chart.

As a reserve, The Lodge comprises open heathland with bracken, heather and

150

grasses. Oaks, Scots pines with a rather open canopy, scattered stands of birches, and some fine old sweet chestnuts predominate; there are also rhododendrons, cedars, black pines and redwoods, with plantations of larch and Douglas fir among others. A shrub garden is planted with berry-bearing species (food for birds), and there is a 'Nature Discovery Room' looking over a bird garden and pond.

One of the characteristics of any successful business larger than one man and his dog is that it spends a lot of time fretting about what to do next. And the more successful a business, the more inclined it is to worry over the future. With its centenary looming, the Society has understandably prescribed for itself not only practical objectives, like recruiting another 100,000 members, but also an heroic dose of speculative navel-gazing.

These activities, like so many touched on during the course of this history, serve a function that is probably more ceremonial than anything else. Much of what is written in the perpetration of five-year, ten-year, even (heaven help us) 100-year plans is, of course, arrant nonsense, or the obvious minutiae of day-to-day, month-to-month, business committed to paper, and therefore it is hoped to posterity, simply because someone's superior has ordained that it is time for a report.

The Society is proud of its achievements to date, and faces the future in as strong a position as any conservation body in the world. But presumably it would be too simple – ceremony would be denied, ritual felt wanting – to say merely: "We hope for the next century to go on doing roughly the same things, roughly as successfully, as we have done for the past century. We propose to survive." But however prolix and ornate the various long-term plans, prognostications, diagnoses and prescriptions, that is what they are going to be saying.

Such exercises, however necessary as ritual, are still inordinately silly, or so it seems to me, at this point in history especially – our own collective history, that is; society's history as against the Society's history. The reasons are, or should be, blindingly obvious even to the initiators and perpetrators of the long-term plans. But I shall spell out those reasons anyway.

Briefly: on current evidence, there are unlikely to be any birds to protect in a hundred years' time. There may in any case be no people to protect them from; if there are any birds, and any people, those people are unlikely to be in a position to afford the luxury of even thinking about the birds except as something to eat, if they are in any condition to catch them. If I am wrong (like the bureaucrats, I too have a contingency plan), and our species has not all but wiped itself out, the result will still be much the same: the degradation of habitats, all habitats, however defined, will have gone so far that what we call conservation today will bear no relation to the activities of our great-grandchildren.

During the latter half of this century there have been several heroic attempts to reverse, halt or at least slow down the process of planetary degradation. It is those efforts, stupefyingly dry in detail but sensational in their implications, which have probably made it possible for me to write this book at all with any likelihood that it would be understood by a general readership. Relatively few people may even now have heard of the Stockholm Conference on Environment in 1972, or the World Conservation Strategy launched eight years later. But many now understand what an ecosystem is; they admit the possibility that the extinction of a species or the destruction of a habitat might be cause for concern, and they can even see the relevance of such considerations to their own mean existence.

Nasty, brutish and short our lives may be; but they are arguably better than no lives at all. It is some such assumption that underlines, for example, organised resistance to the deployment of nuclear weaponry, itself perhaps the ultimate in environmental menace. Natural processes that have run amok because of ruthless (when not merely heedless) overexploitation may grind rather more slowly, but in the end they grind just as small, as any engine of military destruction.

In 1972 the Swedes, alarmed at the devastation acid rain was beginning to work throughout Scandinavia, managed to organise the Stockholm conference in order to put their case before an international agenda; at the same time, delegates took the opportunity to define environmental concerns as a legitimate subject for diplomacy, in large part through the various agencies of the United Nations. In due course, from many of the same sources and for many of the same reasons, the World Conservation Strategy managed to summarise in a few short, relatively readable pages what the human race might be assumed to have learned from its mistakes of the past millennia.

It is far too soon to judge whether the immense bureaucratic convulsion that produced such a masterpiece of concision will have had any practical effect whatsoever, although some of the motions – such as the preparation of various 'National Conservation Strategies' – have been dutifully gone through. But if the Society must concoct a series of targets for the next hundred years, it might as well do the job properly, and the World Conservation Strategy says it all rather more succinctly than any document likely to emerge from The Lodge. I am not saying for a moment that I believe the Strategy, on past human form, is workable. But we might as well face doomsday with an appropriate catechism on our lips. To wit:

> "The aim of the World Conservation Strategy is to achieve the three main objectives of living resource conservation: to maintain essential ecological processes and life-support systems; to maintain genetic diversity; to ensure the sustainable utilisation of species and ecosystems."

We have come full circle, then, to where I started: when the worst is over, if there are any survivors, someone, somewhere will of course be scurrying about performing some benign activity in connection with such lesser species as may have also survived. The impulse, at least, of conservation will abide, even as the objects of conservation subside into the cinders of the hereafter together with their persecutors, like the reflexes which cause a corpse to carry on twitching after death.

I would not dream of trying to dissuade the faithful of the Society from carrying on with their centenary work. But such are *my* long-term plans, and I'm sticking to them.

Meanwhile, I should like to carry to our collective grave, or more likely, crematorium, agreeable memories of lunch-time at The Lodge: a hearty, low-cost meal, served in a small but distinctly elegant dining room, with an excellent view on to the grounds. In fine weather, you can watch the employees of the Society strolling round in this sempiternally English setting, watching each other, watching the birds, and there is as much coffee as you want. Sometimes, just sometimes, it does all seem a bit too good to be true.

152

Roy Dennis, RSPB Regional Officer North Scotland (left) and the late George Waterston (right) greet a white-tailed sea eagle, a chick imported from Norway as part of the Nature Conservancy Council's project begun in 1975 to reintroduce the species on Rhum.

George, who played such an important part in "Operation Osprey" in the 1950s, died in 1979, but warden David Sexton wrote in Birds *magazine "Late in March 1985, our round-the-clock guard ... began. ... At dawn on 4 May, the female was restless ... she bent her head into the nest as if offering food. ... The CB radio crackled into life. The signal was poor but the message was clear. 'I think we're both daddies!'" The sea eagle had bred in Great Britain for the first time in 70 years.*

153

100 YEARS

The Royal Society for the Protection of Birds is the charity that takes action for wild birds and the environment. The threats are real – river pollution, destruction of heathlands, moorlands, hedgerows and estuaries, and illegal shooting, trapping and poisoning of wildlife. The RSPB is fighting these threats, but your support is vital. Birds are everyone's concern. By protecting them we ensure a healthy environment for ourselves and our children. Whatever your age, wherever you live you can join in the action for birds. Do you enjoy and care about the countryside enough to support us?

The RSPB
- Buys large tracts of land as nature reserves.
- Works closely with landowners to create a better countryside.
- Fights damaging developments that threaten wildlife.
- Protects our rarest breeding birds.
- Brings the experience of wildlife to people of all ages.
- Has expertise which is frequently sought by government.

IAN PRESTT
Director General RSPB

154

The RSPB's Patron is Her Majesty the Queen.

Here, the Society's Director General Ian Prestt presents conductor and arranger Louis Clark to Her Majesty at a Royal Gala Concert in 1982.

155

Appendix 1   Chronology

1889   Foundation of Society for the Protection of Birds in Didsbury, Manchester
1891   Society's Secretary now based in London
1898   Society's first Christmas card printed
1902   Watchers' Fund started
1903   Bird Notes and News first published
1904   Royal Charter granted
1921   Importation of Plumage (Prohibition) Act
        Ulster society for the Protection of Birds founded
1931   Acquisition of first reserves – Dungeness, Kent; and Eastwood, Stalybridge
        Wild Birds Protection Legislation (N Ireland)
1943   Junior Bird Recorders' Club founded as junior branch of RSPB
1947   Avocet returns to breed at Minsmere and Havergate
        Minsmere acquired as a reserve
1949   Havergate acquired as a reserve
1952   Black-tailed godwit returns to breed at Ouse Washes
1954   Duchess of Portland, RSPB's first President, dies
        Protection of Birds Act passed
        Regional office established in Scotland
1958   Osprey returns to breed at Loch Garten. Nest is robbed
1959   Osprey breeds successfully at Loch Garten
1961   RSPB moves headquarters from London to the Lodge, Sandy, Bedfordshire
1963   Peter Conder becomes Secretary of the Society (title later changed to Director)
        Ruff returns to breed at Ouse Washes
1965   Young Ornithologists' Club founded (developed from JBRC)
1966   Beached Bird Survey commences
1967   Second Protection of Birds Act passed
        Torrey Canyon oil-spill disaster – at least 10,000 birds killed
        Regional office established in Northern Ireland following merger with RSPB
        Appeal for £100,000 to buy four properties: Loch Leven, Ynys-hir, Gwenffrwd,
            Ouse Washes
        Snowy owl breeds on Fetlar
1969   First RSPB members' group established – in Epping Forest
1971   Regional office established in Wales
        Financial recession hits Society – July/August issue of Birds not published
1975   Ian Prestt becomes Director
        Save a Place for Birds Appeal
1976   Endangered Species (Import/Export) Act
1978   National outcry over proposal to develop Ribble estuary
1979   Silver Meadows Appeal
1981   Wildlife and Countryside Act passed, replacing the Protection of Birds Acts
1982   Woodland Appeal
1984   100th reserve acquired – The Wood of Cree
1985   Eric Morecambe Memorial Appeal launched
        White-tailed eagle breeds for the first time in nearly 70 years
        Wildlife Order (N Ireland)
        Nature Conservation and Amenity Lands Order (N Ireland)

Chapter 1
Galsworthy, John. *For Love of Beasts*. RSPB Leaflet No 69 (1912).
Samstag, Tony. 'Stick that in your manifesto: Notes towards a politics of environment.' *World Conservation Strategy Occasional Paper No 4*. World Wildlife Fund (1983-84).
Sheail, John. *Nature in Trust, the history of nature conservation in Britain*. Blackie (1976).
Turner, E S. *All Heaven in a Rage*. Michael Joseph (1964).

Chapter 2
Basset, Philippa. 'A list of the historical records of the Royal Society for the Protection of Birds.' Centre for Urban and Regional Studies, Birmingham University, and Institute of Agricultural History, Reading University (1980).
Collinge, W E. *The National Importance of Wild Birds*. RSPB Leaflet No 84 (1927).
Doughty, Robin W. *Feather Fashions and Bird Preservation: A study in Nature Protection*. University of California Press (1975).
Hammond, Nicholas. 'Conservation and sister organisations: Royal Society for the Protection of Birds.' *In* Hickling, R, ed. *Enjoying Ornithology: a celebration of fifty years of The British Trust for Ornithology 1933-1983*. (BTO) T & A D Poyser, pp 158-164 (1983).
Hudson, W H. *A Linnet for Sixpence*. RSPB Leaflet No 50 (1904).
Hudson, W H. *OSPREY or Egrets and Aigrettes*. RSPB Leaflet No 3 (1986).
Lemon, Mrs Frank. 'The Story of the RSPB.' *Bird Notes and News*, Vol XX, Nos 5-8 (1943).
Little, Mrs Archibald. *Our Pet Herons*. RSPB Leaflet No 35 (1900).

Chapter 3
Rook, Dorothy. 'Protecting Britain's Birds.' *Birds*, Vol 1, No 4, pp 65-69, RSPB (1966) (reprinted as leaflet 1969).
'The Plumage Trade.' *Bird Notes*, Vol XXVI, No 6 (1955).

Chapter 4
Appeal for the Birds. RSPB Leaflet No 101 (1942).
Bird Notes and News, Vol X, No 5, RSPB (1923).
Eric Morecambe Memorial Appeal brochure (1985).
Hammond, Nicholas. 'Artists and Animals.' *BBC Wildlife* magazine (September, 1986).

Chapter 5
Brown, Philip, and Waterston, George. *The Return of the Osprey*. Collins (1962).
Hammond, Nicholas (ed). *RSPB Nature Reserves*. RSPB (1983).

Samstag, Tony. 'Where the Joy of Watching.' *The Times* (2-8 October, 1982).
Smart, Nicholas, and Andrews, John. *Birds and Broadleaves Handbook*. RSPB (1985).

Chapter 6
Hammond, Nicholas. 'Putting Order into Law.' *Birds*, Vol 8, No 1, pp 50-53. RSPB (1980).
Housden, Stuart. 'Wildlife in Westminster.' *Birds*, Vol 9, No 1, pp 50-52. RSPB (1982).

Chapter 7
Andrews, John. 'Joining Forces with Forestry.' *Birds*, Vol 9, No 1, pp 22-23. RSPB (1982).
Cadbury, C J. 'Silent Death: the destruction of birds and mammals through deliberate misuse of poisons in Britain.' RSPB (1980).
Mason, Christopher. 'Problems in Broadland.' *Birds*, Vol 7, No 2, pp 32-35. RSPB (1978).
Porter, Richard, and Everett, Michael. 'Raptor Round-up.' *Birds*, Vol 9, No 7, pp 24-28, and Vol 8, pp 24-28. RSPB (1983).
Ratcliffe, Derek. *The Peregrine*. T & A D Poyser (1980).
Tompkins, Steve. 'Birds, Conifers and Money.' *Birds*, Vol 11, No 3, pp 22-27. RSPB (1986).
Tyler, Stephanie. 'Acid Water and River Birds.' *RSPB Conservation Review*, No 1. RSPB (1987).
Marine Oil Pollution and Birds. RSPB (1979).

Chapter 8
Robinson, Peter. 'A Well-marked Pair.' *Bird Detective*. Elm Tree Books/Hamish Hamilton (1982).

Chapter 9
Educational Leaflets. RSPB.

Chapter 10
Inskipp, T P. *All Heaven in a Rage: a study into the importation of Birds into the United Kingdom*. RSPB (1975).
Inskipp, T P, and Thomas, G J. *Airborne Birds: a further study into the importation of birds into the United Kingdom*. RSPB (1976).
RSPB Leaflets on Ghanaian project.

Chapter 11
RSPB Leaflets, other internal documents and correspondence.
The World Conservation Strategy: living resource conservation for sustainable development, Kogan Page (1980).
Source material has often been used in more than one chapter; first references only are listed.

Index

Index